102 Things
You Ought'a Know About

your
rights
at**work**

Shawn Sher

Introduction—Making it Easy to Understand

The world of work can be a very muddled place, especially when you're trying to understand what your organization can and cannot do, or what you can and cannot do in enforcing your rights. So, whether it comes down to you questioning your organization's rationale for laying you off, disciplining you for under performance, or even intimidating you for reporting a safety violation, getting the answer can be a pretty laborious and mind-numbing effort.

Legal references and lawyers don't usually help in this process of giving you straight answers either. When you see a lawyer, you seek clarification or answers that you can readily grasp or understand. Unfortunately, with the confluence of fifty state laws, numerous more city ordinances, federal laws, and civil rights statutes, your lawyers probably read straight from a legal reference or quoted a law in attempting to explain things to you. If you've ever been read a law or statute, you'll appreciate the point I am getting at. You feel befuddled, more at a loss than before your discussion.

It is common knowledge that the legal profession doesn't have a vested interest in making things easy to understand. Why should they when they can make a lot more money from making things sound and look more complicated? And the more complicated it appears, the more likely you are to surrender your fate and *wallet*, feeling that this problem best be left in the hands of experts. But the truth is the law isn't rocket science. While not exactly effortless to understand, it can be more easily put across and this is what this book promises.

102 Things You Ought' a Know About Your Rights At Work is written precisely with one aim at heart: to inform you of your rights at work minus the legal mumbo jumbo. It isn't designed for the lawyer, but the layman in you, the one that craves simplicity, clearly defined explanations, and easy reading. You'll even find humorous cartoons included throughout the book in punctuating the message that employment law can be explained in an easy to comprehend and entertaining manner.

In this book, you will find 102 specific ways in which you can use the law in your favor. Starting with the Fair Labor Standards Act (FLSA), it takes you through what your employer can and cannot do with regard to your rights concerning minimum wage, work hours and overtime.

The next topic explored is discrimination. As three quarters of the U.S. population falls under the definition of a "protected group," there is a 75 percent likelihood that you are protected under discrimination laws in one form or another, be it on the basis of your sex, age, religion, marital status, sexual orientation, disability or ethnicity. Particular emphasis is accordingly devoted to letting you know the criteria for claiming discrimination, what you can do when you feel you've been discriminated against, and how you can go about asserting your rights.

Following this, the concept of employment "at will" is discussed where this book explores circumstances where you may be able to challenge your employer's decision to terminate or fire you. It also here describes situations where your employer may have unwittingly, via his conduct, usurped his right to terminate employees "at will." Finally, your rights with regard to privacy, vacation, medical, whistleblower protection as well as unemployment insurance rights are covered.

To complement the 102 nuggets of information, a segment solely devoted to important employment law related court decisions is included. Here, you'll find twenty two important court decisions covering a variety of employer-employee dispute areas. These include awards on the Fair Labor Standards Act, age discrimination, sex discrimination, Americans with Disabilities Act, employment "at will," Sarbanes Oxley, freedom of speech, "noncompete" agreements, and union issues. These court decisions are also stripped off much of its legalese in ensuring they can be easily understood while giving you direct insight into the kind of protection you can expect from the courts.

It is my hope that you will profit from this book to advance your employment prospects as well as to protect it. I'd also like to take this opportunity to encourage you to always think twice before committing to legal action against your employer. Lawsuits are expensive and do consume a huge amount of emotional and mental energy. In using this information constructively, you may well find it more beneficial to educate and encourage your employer to take corrective action instead of suing him.

The Boss

What Part of Etc, Etc, Etc, Don't You Understand?

Final thought before you begin your journey with this book: play fair and use the wisdom gained wisely.

Some Important Court Decisions You Oughta Know About

Table of Contents

18. Your local union has rights to collect "service fees" from you despite your not being a member.

19. "Noncompete" agreements must be specific, reasonable, and fair to the employee.

20. Your pension fund can't vary your pension terms once you've retired.

21. Your employer may have created exceptions to its "employment at will" policy.

22. Same-sex harassment is still protected under Title VII coverage.

FLSA
Fair Labour Standards Act

I. YOUR EMPLOYER CANNOT ESCAPE THE FLSA

" WE'D LIKE TO PAY YOU WHAT YOU'RE WORTH TOO, FOCKER. UNFORTUNATELY, WE MUST CONFORM TO THE MINIMUM WAGE LAW."

The Fair Labor Standards Act relates to wages and work hours. It is under this act that issues like the minimum wage rate, overtime, and working hours are covered. The FLSA states that all employers engaged in interstate commerce with sales of at least US$500,000 are covered under this act. Where things get complex lies in determining whether an employer:

1. is engaged in interstate commerce, or
2. produces goods for sale in interstate commerce.

This has been largely settled via recent court decisions which have clarified that even sending mail to another state or making a telephone call to another state would be sufficient to show that the employer is engaged in "interstate commerce." The effect of this clarification is that most employers are covered under the act—and chances are so is yours.

2. HOW DO I FILE A COMPLAINT?—FLSA VIOLATIONS

First, you need to determine what your complaint is about. If your complaint concerns issues pertaining to your employer not complying with minimum wage requirements, work hours, or overtime laws, your complaint is an FLSA (Fair Labor Standards Act) violation which falls under the arena of your state department of labor. You have a time limit of two years to file your complaint with your state Department of Labor (three if the violation is willful on your employers' part).

The FLSA will then investigate your complaint and, if it finds your complaint is merited, conduct an audit of your employers' wage policies. You can request anonymity when filing your complaint. If any violation is identified, you and anyone else who has suffered from the FLSA violation stands to earn back pay and liquidated damages (equal to the back pay awarded), plus attorney and court fees.

If the FLSA declines to pursue your case, you still have the option of a private lawsuit against your employer.

3. YOU STAND TO EARN DOUBLE FOR FLSA VIOLATIONS

If you report an FLSA violation to your state department of labor (DOL), it has a duty to investigate your complaint and, if it finds the complaint has merits, proceed to conduct an audit of your company's wage policies. An audit of an organization's wage policies are what employers fear most, because if the state DOL finds that your employer has violated wage laws, you *and* everyone else who is underpaid are entitled to back pay, attorney and court costs, and "liquidated" damages—which will equal the amount of back pay awarded.

The award of liquidated damages for any FLSA violation is automatic. So, if you win your case, you automatically will earn double what your employer owes you!

4. HOW MUCH MONEY CAN I WIN?—FLSA VIOLATION

If your employer is found to have violated the Fair Labor Standards Act, you can stand to earn:

1. Your back pay limited to two years. If the violation is willful, you can be compensated up to three years' back pay.
2. Damages equal to the amount of back wages awarded under item 1.
3. Your attorney fees and court costs.

5. YOU ARE STILL COVERED UNDER THE FLSA EVEN IF YOU OWN SHARES IN YOUR ORGANIZATION

Generally, the law stipulates that if you perform manual work and earn a weekly wage of less than $455, you are covered under the FLSA. However, if you manage other staff or perform administrative, creative, information technology, or other intellectually related work such as accounting, law, or engineering, you are exempted from the FLSA provision.

In regard to owning shares with your employer, you are still covered under FLSA provisions as long as your work is largely manual in nature; you earn less than $455; and you are not actively engaged in your company's management. On these grounds, employee share option schemes do not exonerate the employer from having to comply with FLSA rules.

6. YOU MAY AT TIMES EXCEED THE TWO-YEAR FLSA TIME LIMIT

The FLSA stipulates that an employee lodging an FLSA complaint has 2 years. Otherwise, the statute of limitations is invoked. However, the courts have ruled that all an employee has to do is use the guideline of two years from the last date the violation occurred. For instance, assume your organization has been violating state overtime laws in underpaying you for the last five years. In this scenario, you haven't lost your FLSA entitlement yet, as all you need to show is that your employer had underpaid you anytime in the last two years. However, as your back pay is limited to two years (three years for willful violations), prolonging your complaint beyond two or three years means you lose out.

7. YOUR COMPANY CAN'T VARY THE START OF THE WORKWEEK

Under the FLSA, an employer is required to pay overtime of one and a half times regular pay to its employees for overtime in excess of forty hours in a week. The FLSA also allows employers to determine when the start of the workweek is for purposes of determining when overtime needs to be paid. However, once decided, the FLSA also requires consistency from employers, and your employer cannot change when the start of each workweek is for purposes of minimizing overtime payments. So, your employer, in tweaking its overtime exposure, can't tell you this week that the workweek begins Monday, then change the start of the following workweek to Wednesday before changing the start of the workweek after that to Thursday.

8. YOU NEED NOT BE COVERED BY THE NLRA TO BE PROTECTED

Fret not about whether union membership is a prerequisite for protection under the National Labor Relations Act (NLRA). All employees or employers engaged in interstate commerce (we went through this under the definition of what interstate commerce is under the FLSA section) are automatically protected under the NLRA, whether or not they are a member of the union.

Being a
contractor

9. INDEPENDENT CONTRACTORS HAVE RIGHTS, TOO

"You Gotta Love This Government Contract Job! Every Morning I'll Paint The Word 'Open' On The Window, Then Every Evening, I Wash It Off And Paint The Word 'Close'"

You apply for a job and are told bluntly by your prospective employer that the only way he will consider any form of a working relationship is if you avail yourself to work for him as an independent contractor. There are a number of reasons why your prospective employer wants you classified as an independent contractor, and this includes enabling him to avoid:

1. paying unemployment insurance taxes for you;
2. having workers compensation insurance to cover you; and
3. paying for your medical insurance and other employment benefits.

Furthermore, independent contractors are also not covered by Title VII of the Civil Rights Act, which prohibits hiring, firing, or promoting on the basis of your race, color, religion, sex, or national origin.

An independent contractor is someone who follows a trade, business, or profession that is independent of the person employing him, i.e., he is his own boss. For example, assume you are a taxation consultant hired by an organization to help manage its taxation issues over a six-month project. The employer in this case may have control over the result of your work, but since you have "control" over the means and methods to accomplish this, you fall under the definition of an independent contractor.

The problem, however, lies in determining who is in "control," and employers have been known to take advantage of this uncertainty to assert that an employee is an independent contractor, depriving the employee of statutory protection and benefits. The law, however, favors you, and if you can show that

1. you worked normal working hours,
2. your employer retained control over you work, i.e., you had someone directly supervising your work, or
3. you were paid a fixed rate at a regular interval,

the courts will award you compensation in the form of any owed benefits that had been denied to you, including any medical, unemployment, and retirement benefits that you would have been entitled to as an "employee" of that organization. So, remember—just because your employer asserts that you are an "independent contractor" doesn't necessarily mean you are, and you can challenge this.

10. AN INDEPENDENT CONTRACTOR—KNOW THE EIGHT-QUESTION "COMMON LAW" TEST

The issue of whether you are an independent contractor or an employee is an important and complex one. Quite simply, if you're an independent contractor, you're on your own out here with no employer's Social Security contributions, workers' compensation insurance, or medical insurance. You have to bear this on your own.

Companies naturally like you to be labeled an "independent contractor," as this will reduce their total wage bill. However, this doesn't mean that all your employer has to do is get you to change your status from an employee to an independent contractor at his whim. The law protects you here by applying the "common law" test (used by the Internal Revenue Service) in determining your status. Eight questions are asked under this test:

1. Did you perform the work on company property on set work hours?
2. Did you get any training on how to do the job?
3. Is your working relationship continual?
4. Are you paid by the hour, week, and month, or are you paid upon completion of the job?
5. Do you work exclusively for one company?
6. Does the company provide you with tools and equipment, or do you bring your own?
7. Are you reimbursed for your travel and business expenses?
8. Is there any contractual liability if you quit?

These eight questions are designed essentially to determine overall the degree of "control" the employer has over you in the working relationship. The more control your employer has, the more likely you are an employee—regardless of how he may currently label you.

Your
wages

11. AVOIDING MINIMUM WAGE IS A NO-NO

One common strategy adopted by employers in paying less than the minimum wage requirement is to average your wages. If you are paid on an hourly basis, remember that your employer cannot pay you less for some hours and more for others during the workweek, even though it may average or equal the minimum wage. Each hour you work must meet the minimum wage required under the law (currently at $7.25 per hour). Similarly, if you are paid a fixed rate, your amount of fixed wages divided by the number of hours you work has to average at least the minimum wage.

12. KNOW WHAT YOUR EMPLOYER CANNOT DEDUCT FROM YOUR WAGES

While all state laws require employers to withhold income taxes, Social Security taxes, and court attachments to pay debts, spousal or child support from wages, most states also specifically prohibit deductions for the following:

1. any inducements to cover shortages, breakages, losses, or thefts caused or committed by customers;
2. any inducements in order to have you keep your job;
3. medical expenses for work-related injuries; and
4. any medical exams required by the employer.

13. DON'T DOCK MY PAY, PLEASE!

Can your employer dock your pay for petty violations such as being late for work? No, your employer cannot dock your pay for coming in late if it causes your pay for the hours you work to fall below the minimum wage. Furthermore, if your employer wants to dock your pay for being late, he must not allow you to work during that time. For example, assume you arrive at 8:07 a.m. for your 8 a.m. shift. In this situation, your employer cannot put you to work and not pay you for the time worked between 8:07 a.m. and 8:30 a.m. He can, however, tell you not to work and come back at only 8:30 a.m. to start your shift.

Your employer also cannot dock your pay for any cash shortfall, breakages, or lost items if the reduction results in your taking home less than minimum wage.

14. YOU'RE ENTITLED TO OVERTIME NO MATTER HOW MUCH YOU EARN IF YOU PERFORM MANUAL WORK

If you perform work involving repetitive operations requiring the use of your hands, physical skill, and energy, your employer *must* pay you overtime and cannot escape the provisions of the Fair Labor Standards Act (FLSA). Manual work also extends to nonmanagement employees who work as carpenters, electricians, mechanics, plumbers, iron workers, and so on.

However, if you prepare research reports, for example, and your work involves a lot of typing, you won't fall within the definition of a manual worker, because, while the typing is repetitive and manual in nature, the key agent involved here is your brain. Think of it this way: Say you're told by your employer to paint all four walls of the conference room in white. This work is considered manual work. However, if your employer tells you to create a sculpture or painting in beautifying this same conference room, the work involved isn't manual work, because the key agent you are using is your creative ability, i.e., brainwork, with your hands being incidental to this process.

Working hours

15. COFFEE BREAKS, WAITING TIME, AND TRAVEL TIME ARE PART OF YOUR WORK HOURS

"Some Of Us In The Office Feel You Might Be Abusing the Break Room"

Here's good news. Your employer has to pay you for your coffee breaks. But before you rush out from the office with this rose-colored vision of your head and bum perched comfortably on that favorite leather couch of yours at Starbucks, sipping your favorite latte, there's a catch. You only have twenty minutes! Any coffee break in excess of twenty minutes means your employer is entitled to regard the excess as nonwork hours. And this includes the travel time to get to and from Starbucks. So, if you can squeeze all this in within twenty minutes, your coffee break is on the company!

If you are asked to wait around by your employer, be it to be on standby or on call, this is regarded as working time, which means you must be paid for it. In regard to travel, if you're asked to travel to another location from your normal place of work, you are entitled to be paid. For example, if you're asked to fly from New Jersey to Miami to attend to a client, the time it takes to get you there is considered work time, and you have to be paid for those hours.

16. GIVING COMPENSATORY TIME OFF FOR OVERTIME WORK IS ILLEGAL

Compensatory time, often called "comp time," is when an employer gives an employee who has worked overtime time off, instead of paying him or her the overtime. Private employers, i.e., nongovernmental state or local employers, are not allowed to give comp time in place of paying overtime. So, if your employer tells you that you can take five hours off tomorrow in recognition of the five hours of overtime you worked today, you are entitled to lodge a complaint under the Fair Labor Standards Act (FLSA) with your state department of labor, *even if you signed a waiver* authorizing your employer to give you comp time off in lieu of paying overtime. Remember, any waiver that contravenes the law will be disregarded by the state and courts.

Sexual
Harassment

17. YOUR EMPLOYER CAN BE HELD VICARIOUSLY LIABLE FOR SEXUAL HARASSMENT

"Vicarious liability" means that your employer can be held liable (i.e., you can sue for damages) if one of its managers, supervisors, or staff members sexually harasses you. Vicarious liability is broken into two distinct categories explained below:

1. If your superior's harassment results in you being fired, not hired, demoted, not promoted, or having your wages/benefits reduced, your employer is 100 percent vicariously liable.

2. If your harassment involves teasing, crude comments or off-hand remarks that are not extremely serious, your employer could limit or even avoid vicarious liability if he can prove that he took reasonable steps to prevent sexual harassment at the workplace and provided for corrective action. This includes having a clearly published sexual harassment policy which provides for impartial investigation and immediate corrective action. If you can, however, demonstrate that the teasing or crude remarks had escalated into creating a "hostile working environment" which you raised to your employer and which was not corrected, the employer will be held vicariously liable.

18. WHAT ISN'T SEXUAL HARASSMENT

"No I Don't Call It Sexual Harassment, I Call It Casual Friday!"

While having your boss grab you from behind and force his lips on yours is clearly sexual harassment, what about situations where you find yourself in a work culture where your male colleagues in particular use sexually coarse and vulgar language when referring to females, and you're a female?

The courts have stated that in order to constitute sexual harassment, the remark uttered must be one that a reasonable person would find objectively and subjectively offensive. Doesn't help much, does it? Let's try and simplify this criterion.

What the courts are, in essence, stating is that in order to make out a case for sexual harassment, the key lies in the "context" and "circumstances" in which the offending remark was used. If, for example, you're the only female machinist in your shift and find that you are subjected to your male colleagues grunting and pantomiming sex each time you bend down to pick up your tools, you probably have a strong case for sexual harassment. But if you're part of the writing team for a movie script that centers around love and sex in the modern age, having your colleagues talk openly about the female anatomy isn't sexual harassment. Neither is walking into your boss's office to find him ogling at a topless image on his computer screen, which he promptly closes. You may find it offensive and rude, but it doesn't necessarily mean you've been sexually harassed!

19. SAME-SEX SEXUAL HARASSMENT IS A TITLE VII CIVIL RIGHTS VIOLATION

Male-on-male sexual harassment, be it in the form of a male superior asking for sexual favors from his male staff or a group of men verbally abusing another man by calling him queer and threatening him with physical assault, are forms of sexual harassment protected under Title VII of the Civil Rights Act.

Some years ago, the U.S. Supreme Court, in *Oncale v. Sundowner Offshore Services Inc.*, held that the plaintiff employee (who worked offshore on an oil platform in the Gulf of Mexico) was entitled to claim sexual harassment when he was subjected to sex-related, humiliating actions by three of his male colleagues in the presence of the rest of the crew, including assaulting him in a sexual manner and threatening him with rape.

So, whether it's male on male or female on female harassment, Title VII protection applies.

20. THE FLIP SIDE—YOU CAN SUE FOR DEFAMATION IF YOU'RE FALSELY ACCUSED

What happens if you find yourself on the wrong end of a sexual harassment allegation? Maybe a co-worker with a romantic proposal that you rebuffed decides to heap scorn and retaliates by accusing you of sexual harassment. Do you have any rights? Are you expected to sit glum and still, await the results of the internal investigation, and hope for the best, that you are cleared? The unfortunate reality is the moment you are accused of sexual harassment, you are probably "guilty until proven innocent," at least in some of your colleagues' eyes. Here's what you can do (provided, of course, you are innocent!):

1. Gather your own evidence. You will need to show that the investigation process undertaken by your employer was flawed in order to sue them.
2. You can also sue your accuser for false accusation of sexual harassment.
3. Finally, consider a defamation suit—you have this right.

Discrimination

21. ALMOST EVERY AMERICAN IS COVERED UNDER TITLE VII

The Equal Employment Opportunity Commission, or EEOC, is where you go to file your complaint of discrimination. Think of the EEOC as the police department that enforces Title VII of the Civil Rights Act, the act that deals with discrimination. Title VII essentially states that an employer may not refuse to hire you (when applying for a job) or discriminate against you (once you have your job) because of your race, color, religion, or national origin. Title VII is also supported by other antidiscrimination laws, such as the Age Discrimination in Employment Act, Equal Pay Act, and the Americans with Disabilities Act.

When originally conceived, these laws were developed for "protected" groups, usually minorities. However, the reality of today's dynamic, multicultural society structure in America means that unless you are an under-forty, white, agnostic, heterosexual male with no discernible national origin or handicap, you probably have potential recourse with the EEOC. Combine this with the issue of "reverse discrimination"—meaning that you can't be discriminated against because you are *not* a member of a "protected" group—and you can imagine what an explosive, fertile minefield this arena of discrimination at work is—and what a headache it represents to your employer.

22. AGE DISCRIMINATION LAWS: YOU HAVE RIGHTS DESPITE SIGNING A WAIVER

You've probably heard of a story like this: An employer walks into a long-serving employee's room, matter-of-factly tells him the organization is dissatisfied over his work performance, and then offers the stunned employee an easier way to resolve the problem— "Why not retire early?"

The employee is then offered a severance pay if he agrees to go early. With this severance pay, comes a letter (called a waiver) in which the employee gives up his right to sue the organization, and he's expected to sign in exchange for the severance payout.

Now assuming the employee signs this waiver, is this the end of the road for him? Has he lost his rights to sue?

Not necessarily. The courts have ruled that a waiver may not be considered valid in the eyes of the law unless:

1. the agreement or waiver is in writing and easy to understand;
2. it addresses the employee's ADEA (Age Discrimination in Employment Act) rights;
3. the employee receives something in excess of what the law or company policy provides;
4. it advises the employee of his/her right to consult an attorney;
5. the employee is given at least twenty-one days to consider the offer (forty-five days if the offer is made to a group/class of employees); and
6. the agreement can be revoked seven days after it is executed.

So, in short, unless your employer pays you in excess of what the law or company policy provides, informs you of your ADEA rights, including your right to consult an attorney, and gives you reasonable time to think and even revoke the agreement, the waiver is invalid, and you can still take legal action!

23. YOU CAN CLAIM "DAMAGES" FOR CIVIL RIGHTS VIOLATIONS

If you can prove that you suffered intentional discrimination by your employer, the revisions made under the Civil Rights Act of 1991 now allow you to sue for damages. The amount awarded for damages is, however, limited to the size of your employer's workforce and is based on the following formula.

Number of Employees	Formula
15 – 200	$50,000
101 – 200	$100,000
201 – 500	$200,000
501 or more	$300,000

This cap on damages is only for cases where discrimination has happened on the basis of sex, religion, or disability. If you are a victim of race or national origin discrimination, there is *no limit* on the amount of damages you can sue for.

24. YOU MAY BE "ADVERSELY IMPACTED" WITHOUT YOUR KNOWING IT

Here's a scenario: Your organization, a restaurant, has a policy stating that all male "serving" staff are to refrain from growing beards. According to your company, the reason for this policy is for hygiene purposes. On the surface, this policy sees neutral or impartial. However, what happens if Muslims, Jews, or Sikhs are affected by this policy due to their religious beliefs or practices that encourage the growth of facial hair as a sign of piety?

Another scenario: What happens if it is part of a company's preemployment routine to conduct physical strength tests on all prospective employees? Here, while appearing neutral, female job seekers could contend that the test "adversely impacts" their chances of securing the job.

"Adverse impact" refers to situations where a company's policy or work rule, despite appearing neutral on the surface, has a disproportionately negative impact on a protected group.

To prove adverse impact, the job seeker or employee will, however, have to show proof (known as the "burden of proof") that the employer's practice/policy/rule had resulted in him or his protected group being unfairly discriminated against. Recall that a "protected group" refers to any class of employees that could feel potentially discriminated against on the grounds of race, age, sex, ethnicity, sexual orientation, disability, color, or marital status—in effect, at least three quarters of the U.S. population.

25. GETTING THE EEOC ON YOUR SIDE

The Equal Employment Opportunity Commission, or EEOC, is typically swamped by so many cases that bringing your case to its attention can itself be quite an onerous journey. However, if you're tempted to give up and think it is better to initiate a civil suit directly (with an attorney), think again. The EEOC, when analyzing a complaint, will classify it into one of three classifications: (1) those with a high prospect for success, i.e., a strong case for discrimination, (2) those with a moderate prospect for success, and (3) those with a small chance of succeeding. They then will allocate their resources accordingly: i.e., those with a high success potential will naturally command more of their attention.

So what should you do if you can't seem to get anywhere on your EEOC complaint? *Try harder.* You should organize all documentation and evidence with the objective of giving the EEOC what it is looking for, like:

1. evidence of "adverse impact" violation if the discrimination is racial or due to ethnicity;
2. evidence of others in your position who were similarly discriminated against because of their age, sex, race, religion, etc.,; and
3. letters, memos, and e-mails sent by the organization supporting your accusations.

Note: Once the EEOC backs you, you have a 90 percent chance of recovering something from your employer.

26. ALL YOU NEED IS TO PROVE THAT YOU WERE DEPRIVED OF YOUR EMPLOYMENT CHANCES

The specter of discrimination usually only enters our mind after we have been short-listed for a vacancy but are eventually not hired because of a Title VII factor, such as our age, race, national origin, religion, etc. In fact, you can still initiate a discrimination suit if you can prove that you were deprived of the opportunity to even be considered for the job because of the employer's discriminatory practice. For instance, say your employer requests that all job applicants go through some physical strength tests as part of its preemployment selection criteria. If you are disabled or female, you could initiate a discrimination lawsuit on grounds that by requiring you to undergo a physical strength test, your employer has in effect deprived you of your chances for the job. You needn't prove that you would have got the job had there not been a physical strength test requirement; you need only prove that the test deprived you of your *chance* of getting it.

The courts have, in the past, ruled that employers guilty of such practices must hire the victim and also contact other former victims to inform them that they will be considered for a similar position if they reapply.

27. YOU DON'T NEED AN EEOC GO-AHEAD IF YOUR PAY RIGHTS HAVE BEEN VIOLATED

In almost all discrimination cases (except one), you need to bring your Title VII Civil Rights Act complaint to the state or federal EEOC first, and only after it declines to file a suit are you entitled to hire a lawyer to initiate your own personal lawsuit. The exception applies to the Equal Pay Act, through which, if you feel you are earning lower pay than a colleague of the opposite sex for performing equal work, you can initiate your lawsuit directly without going through the EEOC. Under the Equal Pay Act, you have two years from the date of the violation to bring your lawsuit. If you can show that the violation is willful, you have three years to file your claim.

28. COMPULSORY ARBITRATION DOESN'T STOP THE EEOC

Clauses in your employment contract stating that compulsory arbitration will be used in settling employee-employer disputes are legal—which means you can't ignore it and file your private lawsuit. However, it doesn't stop the EEOC, which, as a third party, can still proceed with action in cases where illegal discrimination has taken place. So, despite having a compulsory arbitration agreement, you could still initiate your illegal discrimination complaint with the EEOC, which has the right to pursue the case against your employer.

29. BEWARE YOUR EMPLOYER'S "HIGHER JOB LEVEL" EXCUSE

The "adverse impact" rule states that if any hiring or promotion decision has a disproportionate impact on a "protected group" (three quarters of the U.S. population), the organization is guilty of discrimination. The test applied is the four-fifths rule, where if you can show that your organization's hiring/promotion practice results in less than 80 percent (four fifths) of the protected group being hired/promoted, a case for "adverse impact" is made.

Employers are wising up to "adverse impact," and one excuse some employers are using to circumvent adverse impact rules when hiring is to state that their decision criteria tested not only for the current job opening but the next step in the company's promotional ladder. The EEOC has recognized this development and stated that the only way an employer can use the "higher job level" reason if he can prove:

1. that employees for the job position are generally promoted to the higher position within a reasonable time;, and
2. the promotion progression is relatively automatic.

30. WHAT TO DO IF THE EEOC DISMISSES YOUR COMPLAINT

Don't sit there agonizing over the EEOC's decision to dismiss your suit. Being a government bureaucracy, there could be a host of reasons behind their decision, which could include them not clearly appreciating the nature and context surrounding how you were discriminated against. Consult an attorney (you'll find some that will charge you a nominal fee for an initial analysis of your complaint and its prospects for success, and some will charge nothing). But don't dither too long, as the law only gives you ninety days to file your private lawsuit against your employer.

If you don't hear from the EEOC after 180 days from your complaint date, you also have the option to request a right-to-sue letter from the EEOC. If the issue of discrimination is based on age, you can request this right-to-sue letter after sixty days.

31. YOU SHOULDER THE BURDEN OF PROOF

I have looked over your case, and I'm
afraid you don't have a leg to stand on

To prove illegal discrimination, the burden of proving it rests on you, the employee. You will need to show the courts that:

1. you are a member of a protected class; and
2. your employer's practices have resulted in you being adversely treated, adversely impacted, or suffering from a perpetuating past discrimination.

Once you do this, the burden of proof then shifts to your employer, who will now have to prove that the adverse treatment, adverse impact, or perpetuating past discrimination complained of isn't true.

Since you initially shoulder the burden of proof, documentation is important, and you need to keep copies of all your organization's policies and procedures, work rules, letters, and statistical information linked to its Affirmative Action programs. If you are unable to obtain all these types of information, the EEOC has the authority to also inspect your organization's documents, including interviewing the relevant individuals in the organization.

32. THINK CLASS ACTION

The harsh reality surrounding lawsuits is that they are a numbers game in the sense that the more employees there are involved in filing a complaint, the more likely the EEOC, and for that matter any attorney consulted, will take the matter seriously. Attorneys in particular will be far more inclined to pursue a case representing a group of employees, as the potential for compensation is higher. The EEOC too will probably initially provide more attention to a complaint if it involves a group of employees, the bigger the group the better.

So, where you feel that you've been discriminated against, broaden your "lenses" and think who else within the organization is suffering the same fate. It could be that others may quietly be feeling disenfranchised and are themselves waiting for someone to initiate a complaint. The world, as they say after all, is "full of followers, but lacking in leadership." By grouping employees together, you can then file a "class action" suit against your employer, i.e., a suit involving a certain group or class of employees that are alleging discrimination.

33. KNOW THE THREE DIFFERENT TYPES OF DISCRIMINATION

Before you think "discrimination," you will need to see the big picture on how the legal landscape surrounding it works. And you need to start by identifying which of the three classes of discrimination your falls under. The first class of discrimination is called adverse treatment (also known as disparate treatment). Adverse treatment occurs when your employer intentionally treats you differently because of your race, color, religion, ethnicity, age, sex, disability, or any other category protected by law. A female employee always asked to prepare and serve tea (when her male colleagues are never asked to do the same) would be an example of adverse treatment.

The second class or type of discrimination is called adverse impact. Also known as disparate treatment, it occurs typically when an organization's seemingly neutral policy has a disproportionately negative impact on a group of "protected class" employees. For example, an organizational policy prohibiting males from growing beards could be found to be discriminatory toward Jews, Muslims, or Sikhs, whose religions could arguably be said to encourage the growth of facial hair.

The third class of discrimination is called perpetuating past discrimination. Here, past practices and policies of an organization perpetuate discrimination. For instance, if an organization has a mainly white population and usually hires through employee referrals, this could result in more white employees referred for employment, thus perpetuating a past discrimination

34. YOU CAN (NOT) BE FORCED TO SPEAK ENGLISH ONLY

We live in a multicultural environment. English is still and will remain for a long time the main spoken language in this country. Henceforth, can your employer require you to speak only English at work?

No, the EEOC presumes that any requirement for employees to speak only English "all the time" while at work (including lunch time, coffee breaks, etc.) is discriminatory. For instance, while your employer does have a right to request you to speak only in English when dealing with customers, he can't force you to speak only English with your colleagues during your meal or coffee breaks. The criteria for determining whether an employer's requirement for speaking English is discriminatory/nondiscriminatory will essentially depend on the factual context of each situation.

35. YOU ALWAYS HAVE THE "TORT" OPTION

What happens if the EEOC decides not to take up your complaint and sue on your behalf? Or your employer is too small to be covered by the EEOA? Well, you still have the option of a "tort" action against your employer. A tort action is a lawsuit for personal injuries suffered—both physical and emotional. If you are successful in your tort action, you could claim for both compensatory (for the physical and emotional distress you suffered) and punitive damages.

36. YOU CAN OPT FOR A JURY TRIAL

The amendments made under the Civil Rights Act of 1991 also provide that employees pursuing discrimination claims can opt for a jury trial.

What does this mean to you? It means an increased likelihood that, should your case go before a jury trial, your chances to recover damages are higher. Think about the movie *Philadelphia*, with Tom Hanks, and the punitive damages his character was awarded. Juries are more likely to be swayed by emotions, meaning they are more susceptible to be guided by feelings and sentiment; a judge is likely to be more measured, technical, and less sensitive in making decisions.

37. KNOW WHAT YOUR EMPLOYER'S DEFENSE ATTORNEY IS TELLING HIM!

When your employer goes to a defense attorney seeking advice on how to deal with an employee suit, attorneys will typically chart out a series of questions designed to assess the employer's probability of success. Knowing what these questions are can help you a long way in positioning your case. After all, by knowing what your employer's defense will be, you are in a superior position to "plug holes" in your case. So here's the checklist of questions your employer will probably be asked:

1. If your case involves discrimination or an EEOC violation, the attorney will ask your employer to determine who the protected groups are (remember, at least three quarters of the U.S. workforce is in a protected group) and whether any cutbacks or work policies have created an "adverse impact" on these groups.

2. Does your employer have clearly established, written work rules and policies? If yes, then how have these rules and policies been communicated to its employees? The latter question is asked so as to develop a defense to allegations by employees that they were never given a copy of the rules/ policies.

3. If the case involves performance and/or discipline issues, the attorney will ask your employer whether it has an established, written policy for progressive discipline (which usually consists of a verbal warning followed by three writing warnings). This question is particularly relevant, as even companies with clearly defined "employment at will" policies may still be at risk if it is later proven that other employees in the past had been "progressively disciplined," giving rise to the employee's

legitimate expectation to be discharged only for just cause after a disciplinary mechanism had been initiated.

4. With regard to performance and disciplinary issues, did the employer document all performance reviews and disciplinary action taken?

5. Did the employer have a grievance process where employees could appeal their firing? This is important, because if the employer had this process in place and you did not follow it, your employer could argue that you should first adhere to the grievance process prior to initiating your lawsuit!

Imagine what your employer's likely responses will be to these questions, and use this insight to proactively position your case against him.

38. "MIXED MOTIVE" DEFENSE DOESN'T WORK

A "mixed motive" defense has in the past been used by employers to justify their discriminatory treatment. For example, an employer may justify any discrimination on grounds that the employee's performance on the job was so poor that termination was likely going to occur anyway.

The amended Civil Rights Act of 1991 prohibits this, and your employer cannot use more than one factor or reason to justify any discriminatory action. All an employee needs to do is prove that "protected class" status was a factor in the company's discriminatory practice. Essentially, this means your employer cannot support any discriminatory practices initiated against you by bringing up your disciplinary or performance history.

39. IT AIN'T EASY FOR EMPLOYERS TO ESCAPE THE EQUAL PAY ACT

The Equal Pay Act mandates that people be paid equally for doing the same job, whatever their sex may be. This act was initially formed to protect the female gender from unfair pay discrimination because of their sex.

The problem with the act lies in determining what constitutes "equal work."

Many employers expose this difficulty in determining the meaning of the term "equal work or equal worth" by justifying their pay differences using reasons such as:

1.   he was more highly qualified;
2.   he was willing to work overtime; or
3.   he is prepared to put in the extra effort.

If you're a female and find this happening to you, take note of this fact: The courts, in determining whether an employer is justified in awarding high pay to someone, will ask the question, "Is the qualification, extra effort, or over-time work a 'substantial' enough consideration to justify the pay difference?" In short, it will delve deep into understanding the nature and circumstances of the job functions to decipher whether the extra qualifications, effort, and overtime are actually substantial requirements justifying a pay difference or merely a flimsy excuse advanced by your employer to cover his tracks.

Mind you, the Equal Pay Act flows both ways, and if you're a male and you find you're losing out in terms of pay to your female colleagues for what you feel is "equal work," the act applies equally to you.

40. HOW DO I FILE MY COMPLAINT— CIVIL RIGHTS VIOLATION

If you feel you've been discriminated against on the job, your recourse is to bring your complaint to the EEOC. You will be required to file a discrimi-nation charge in writing to your employer detailing your allegations. You may request confidentiality when filing your complaint. For EEOC violations, you have a 180day time limit to file your complaint which runs from the date you were notified of the discriminatory action.

Once you file your complaint, the EEOC will notify your employer of the charge within ten days of you filing it. The federal EEOC will also not act on your complaint for sixty days to give your state or local EEOC agency a chance to act upon it. Once the EEOC commences investigations, it has the authority to inspect your employer's records and question any witnesses. It will then attempt to mediate a settlement. If no settlement is reached, the EEOC will either take legal action on your behalf (if it believes you have a valid case) or issue you a "right-to-sue" notice.

Once you are issued a "right-to-sue" notice, you must initiate your private lawsuit within ninety days.

Note: If the discrimination involves Equal Pay Act violations or age discrimination, you don't need the EEOC's "right-to-sue" letter and can directly initiate your private lawsuit.

41. KNOW YOUR BFOQs

There are exceptions to the Title VII prohibitions, and these fall under the category of Bona Fide Occupational Qualification, or BFOQ. If an employer is able to show that it needs someone of a particular religion, sex, or age due to a genuine business need, it can apply to the EEOC for this BFOQ. However, it is increasingly getting harder to obtain a BFOQ today, particularly those involving age or sex, as in almost all job situations, it can be argued that whether the person is twenty or fifty or whether the person is male or female has little bearing on their ability to perform the job.

One common BFOQ is that religious institutions offering counseling for those interested in embracing their religion may require the counselor to be of that particular faith. So, unless your employer has a genuine reason for requiring a BFOQ, it can't discriminate.

42. ASSERT YOUR RIGHTS TO ENGAGE IN A "PROTECTED CONCERTED ACTIVITY"

A "protected concerted activity" refers to any activity aimed at improving an employee's terms and conditions of employment. This is protected by the National Labor Relations Act (NRLA). For instance, say you compose a letter to your colleagues protesting the company's new sales commission structure and inviting them to share their feelings over it. In this scenario, your employer can't fire you as your protest falls under the heading of "protected concerted activity." The National Labor Relations Board (NLRB) has taken plenty of employers to court and won on behalf of employees who were terminated for engaging in "protected concerted activities." Where successful, the employee(s) stand to be reinstated with back pay plus interest to their former position, and the employer will also be required to post a written notice to all its employees detailing its violation and the remedy!

43. COMPARABLE WORTH VS. THE EQUAL PAY ACT

The Equal Pay Act applies when a man and woman perform the same work but one is paid less that the other. In this situation, the person earning less can pursue a complaint directly under the Equal Pay Act—and even choose to initiate a private lawsuit against the employer without needing EEOC approval.

"Comparable worth" as a concept applies in a situation where a man and woman are performing different jobs *but* the value of their jobs to the organization is the same. For example, a male accounts manager and female research manager perform different job functions but their work is of "comparable worth" in terms of what their functions contribute to the organization, and yet they are paid differently. In this scenario, the worth of their jobs is equal, yet one earns more than the other.

If yours is a comparable worth case, it is better for you to pursue the case as a Title VII civil rights violation using state discrimination laws.

44. YOU'RE STILL COVERED IF YOU'RE WORKING ABROAD

The 1991 Civil Rights Act amendments also extended to United States citizens working for U.S. multinationals in foreign countries. This means that if you are sent abroad, your organization must still comply with the Civil Rights Act requirements as long as these rights do not conflict with local laws.

As discrimination laws are pretty much universally recognized, this means that there is a very strong likelihood that if you are an American working overseas for an American company, your civil rights are still protected.

45. YOU HAVE A RIGHT TO THAT PROMOTION DESPITE YOUR PREGNANCY

"No, I Didn't Get The Promotion Again. It's Hard Building A Career When You're On Maternity Leave Every Few Months..."

Being pregnant doesn't mean your employer can choose not to promote you on grounds that you will be on maternity leave soon. Your rights when pregnant are governed under the Family and Medical Leave Act, which means that if you've been denied that promotion due to pregnancy, you have a strong case for a Title VIII Civil Rights Act violation.

46. FRINGE BENEFITS ARE FOR EVERYONE OR NO ONE

Fringe benefits are the work-related benefits one gets as part of one's contribution to the company. Typically, this comes in the form of health care insurance, retrenchment plans, and paid time off for vacations and medical care. What you need to know about fringe benefits is that your employer cannot cherry-pick whom he wants to offer them to. If he decides to offer a certain category of staff these benefits, then all employees must be offered the same fringe benefits. Otherwise, your employer risks facing a discrimination lawsuit.

47. HOW TO CALCULATE IF ADVERSE IMPACT HAS TAKEN PLACE

The determination of adverse impact can be a bit complicated, as there are many statistical methods for doing so. The easiest way is to use the four-fifths rule, which can be used both internally and externally. Internally, this rule can be used to determine whether the organization's policies and procedures are adversely impacting a protected class. Externally, the rule can be used to compare the organization's workforce with the demographics of the external workforce in determining whether any underutilization of protected classes exists.

To determine whether adverse impact has taken place within the organization, let's use the scenario of your organization choosing to hire one hundred employees. When recruiting for these positions, three hundred people were interviewed, of which 150 where white males, seventy-five were African American females, fifty were Hispanic males, and twenty-five were Asian American females. Out of these interviews, seventy-five white males, fifteen African American, seven Hispanic males and three Asian American females were hired. On a percentage scale, this means that 50 percent of white male Americans were hired, i.e., seventy-five out of 150. For African American females, the selection rate is 20 percent, i.e., fifteen out of seventy-five. For Hispanic males, the rate is 14 percent, i.e., seven out of fifty. For Asian American females, the hiring rate is 12 percent, i.e., three out of twenty-five.

Applying the four-fifths rule to the numbers above, the group of employees with the highest selected rate is used as the base comparison group. As white males were hired 50 percent of the time, they serve as the base comparison group. Applying four fifths to 50 percent means that any other "protected group" should be hired at least 40 percent of the time, and any selection rate less than 40 percent means adverse impact has occurred. In this case, this means all the other protected groups (African American females, Hispanic males, and Asian American females) have been discriminated against or adversely impacted.

The formula to compare whether an organization's internal workforce mirrors the demographics of the external job market is to determine what percentage of the organization's workforce each "protected" group occupies against the external job market demographic. If, for instance, African Americans occupy 25 percent of the labor market, applying the four-fifths rule means that if an organization has less than 20 % (4/5 off 25%) African Americans in its workforce, it has adversely impacted this protected class.

48. YOU DO HAVE PRIVACY RIGHTS

Post 9/11, it seems like all those things we took for granted, such as our rights to anonymity, confidentiality, or privacy, are thrown to the wind. In their place is the government's apparently untrammeled right to pry anywhere it likes into our affairs. In the name of national security this is called.

However, as far as your employer's right to snoop goes, the rules are different. While technology has allowed companies to undertake more and more sophisticated forms of surveillance, they can only do so for legitimate business purposes, such as evaluating customer service, improving productivity, and identifying thefts—and they can only search property/items that are designated as company property. For instance, while your employer may have the right to search your work area, he can't search your wallet, which is your personal, private possession.

49. YOUR MEDICAL AND PERSONNEL RECORDS SHOULDN'T BE KEPT TOGETHER

"Somehow Your Medical Records Got Faxed To A Complete Stranger. He Has No Idea What's Wrong With You Either."

While your personnel files are generally open to anyone who supervises you, senior management as well as human resources, the same latitude and access don't apply to your medical records. The only people who may be given access to your medical records are your immediate superior (if he/she needs to be informed of any disability or condition you suffer from), first aid personnel (where you require emergency treatment), and government officials investigating any ADA (Americans with Disabilities Act) compliance/noncompliance by your employer.

The confidentiality of your medical records is expressly covered by the ADA, which mandates that your medical files must be kept confidentially in a separate file from your personnel records.

So, if your employer leaks out your medical details, he could be in for a "roasting" if you take this matter to court as an invasion-of-privacy complaint.

50. PERSONAL CALLS ARE PERSONAL

Most state laws restrict where an employer can go when monitoring employee's telephone calls. Furthermore, federal law stipulates that while an employer can monitor/listen in to your telephone calls (such as calls on company telephone lines and cell phones given to you by the company), an employer must hang up as soon as he determines/realizes that your call is personal in nature.

51. DETAINING YOU IS UNLAWFUL

A theft occurs in the workplace and you are a suspect. Your employer then tells you that you are required to be detained on the company premises until the police arrive. Can your employer do this?

Well, the answer is no. You are no longer in school, and your employer cannot detain you against your will even on the pretext that he is calling the police in to investigate. If he does detain you against your will, you could take an action of false imprisonment against them.

However, should you leave your workplace during work hours or while under shift, your employer will have the right to discipline you—but limited to the extent of your not being at work during your shift.

52. YOU CAN SAY NO TO LIE DETECTORS

Did you know that the Federal Polygraph Protection Act of 1988 prohibits private sector employers from requiring or requesting employees (even job applicants) to submit to a lie detector test? And, your employer cannot discipline, dismiss, or discriminate against you for your refusal.

There are exceptions, however—and these usually relate to situations involving theft or circumstances where an employer lost money, such as sabotage, misappropriation, and embezzlement. Even then, there are certain conditions imposed by law on your employer in asking you to take a polygraph, and they include:

    1.   The incident investigated must be specific, i.e., it must concern only the theft, embezzlement, misappropriation, sabotage, etc.

2.   You must have had access to the missing property or to the place of the incident at the time the incident took place.
3.   Your employer must be able to show "reasonable cause" or suspicion of your involvement in the incident. The test here on reasonable cause is whether an objective, rational person would have reached a similar conclusion on your involvement.
4.   You must be given written notice of the incident investigated, the reasons you are suspected, and a minimum forty-eight hours' notice prior to the test.

Finally, even after you have taken the test, the employer cannot solely rely on its results as the basis for firing you. It must have other supporting or corroborative evidence to support any termination decision.

Note: If you work for the federal, state, or local government, the Federal Polygraph Protection Act doesn't apply to you. Recent additional exemptions include security companies (who may hire employees for purposes of storing and transferring money or proprietary information) and drug and pharmaceutical companies (limited to jobs where the person involved is in contact with controlled drugs).

53. PROTECT YOUR SPOUSE'S CREDIT RIGHTS

Financial institutions usually require both husband and wife to sign loan papers. However, did you know that under federal regulations, "a creditor shall not require the signature of an applicant's spouse...on the credit instrument if the applicant qualifies under the creditors standards of creditworthiness for the amount and terms of the credit requested."

Let's translate this. What this regulation states is that if you are capable of meeting the bank's/financial institution's eligibility criteria for a loan, your wife/husband needn't be held accountable. It means than only the spouse taking the loan can be held responsible for repayment.

54. YOUR CREDIT REPORT CANNOT BE KEPT IN YOUR EMPLOYMENT FILES

"For show and tell, I've brought individual credit reports of the entire school that I've downloaded from the internet."

You may be unaware of an amendment to the Fair Credit Reporting Act called the Fair and Accurate Credit Transactions Act of 2003 (FACTA). This act provides you with certain guarantees:

1. You have the right to get an annual report on your credit status (*for free*).
2. Your employer cannot keep a copy of your credit report once it has made its employment decision. Once it has decided to hire you, it must be removed from your personnel file.

You may also want to bear in mind that under FACTA, your employer no longer requires your prior consent when contracting with a third party for certain types of allegations, such as misconduct, violation of company policies, or legal violations. Your employer is, however, required to notify you in writing of the findings.

Shawn Sher

Whistle Blowing

55. YOU CANNOT BE FIRED FOR COMPLAINING ABOUT THE WORKPLACE

There is a difference between writing a defamatory message and e-mailing it to all your colleagues within the organization, and raising complaints about workplace issues, such as safety standards, wage violations, or the company's benefits policy. The former is "defamation," which entitles your employer to fire you, while the latter is a "protected activity" under the National Labor Relations Act.

The National Labor Relations Board has held in the past that an employee's actions of, for instance, complaining about the company's vacation policy or safety standards is a "protected activity," and employees fired by their employers for such activities should be reinstated *with* back pay.

56. YOU'RE PROTECTED WHEN YOU REPORT SAFETY VIOLATIONS

The Occupational Safety and Health Act (OSHA) covers minimum standards, practices, and guidelines that employers must adopt in maintaining the health and safety of their employees. If you report a health and safety violation at your workplace to the authorities (with OSHA) and find your employer retaliating (be it by disciplining or firing you), you are protected by whistle-blowing laws that prohibit such discrimination or retaliation. And guess what? If you can prove the retaliation, you may, in addition to back pay, be entitled to damages, including damages for emotional distress.

57. RETALIATION BY YOUR EMPLOYER—HERE'S HOW TO PROVE IT

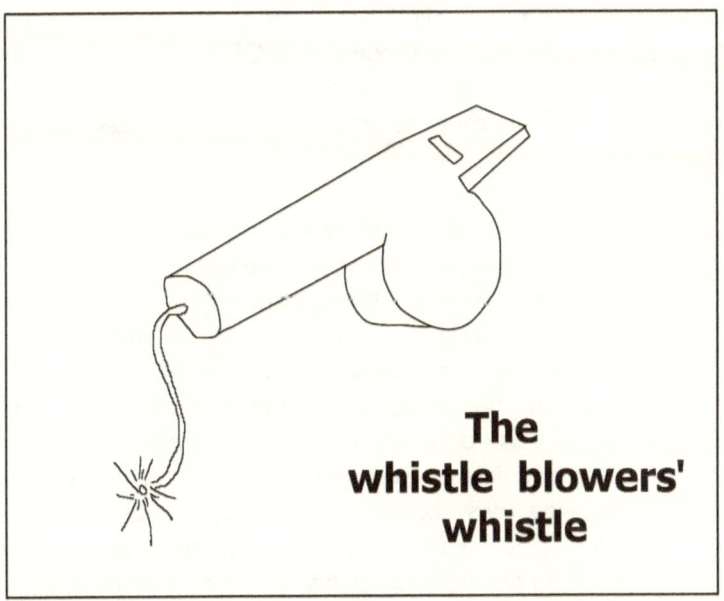

The whistle blowers' whistle

Retaliation by your employer stems from situations where you blow the whistle on your employer or superior, i.e., report any illegal practices, safety violations, or unethical behavior. Hence, the name "whistle-blowing." To prove that you were discharged because you blew the whistle isn't easy, though, as you will need to prove in court that you were fired directly in connection with your whistle-blowing activity. However, rest assured that if you can prove it, there are whistle-blowing laws that protect you. To have the law work for you, there are 3 basic steps:

1. You must prove that you were fired, demoted, sidelined, etc., immediately or soon after you blew the whistle on your employer, i.e., soon after you lodged your complaint.
2. Your employer will have the opportunity to rebut your case by showing that it had a legitimate business reason for firing, demoting, or sidelining you, etc.
3. You must prove that the reason advanced by your employer in step two was just a pretext to cover up the real reason you were fired.

58. A WHISTLE-BLOWERS GUIDE TO PROTECTION

If you can prove you were retaliated against for blowing the whistle on an organization, you stand to win big. When three employees of Lockheed were fired after reporting flaws on the company's C5-B aircraft to management, they sued and won $45.3 million collectively. You could also lose, though, so follow these suggested guidelines to ensure you are protected under whistle-blower laws:

1.   Before you take action, be it to report a safety violation or an accounting fraud, ensure you are *right*.
2.   Give your employer the opportunity to correct the situation first before reporting the matter to the authorities.
3.   If your employer doesn't take corrective action, you can then escalate your complaint to the authorities. *But*, ensure you have all the evidence first. You may even want to consult an attorney first on your probability of protection by whistle-blowing laws should your employer retaliate against your complaint. Ask for company precedents similar to your situation in ensuring you are protected should things go wrong.

59. THE COMPLAINT PROCESS—OSHA VIOLATIONS

If you find your employer is violating any health or safety laws, your recourse lies with the Occupational Safety and Health authorities. You have thirty days to file your violation from the date your employer allegedly violates the safety and/or health law. Once you file your complaint, the law prohibits your employer from discriminating against you, and, should your employer retaliate by firing you for the complaint, you can sue to get your job back, twice the amount of compensation you have lost on your salary/wages, and punitive damages.

60. KNOW HOW SARBANES-OXLEY PROTECTS YOU

In the aftermath of the Enron accounting scandal, the U.S. Congress passed the Sarbanes-Oxley Act in 2002. The act is broad, complex, and continues to evolve as judicial decisions are made. The key points under this act are that:

1. It requires executive certification, i.e., your CEO and CFO typically will need to clarify that your company's financial statements are correct.

2. Employees get whistle-blower protection if they report any securities regulations.

3. It introduces certain blackout periods where employees cannot make certain transactions within their defined contribution plans. The employer is also required to provide thirty days' advance written notice of these blackout periods to its employees.

Interview Stage

61. SAYING NO TO A PREEMPLOYMENT DRUG TEST

Your employer cannot require you to take a drug test as a precondition for considering you for employment. He must offer you the job and state that your employment offer is conditional on you passing a drug test. Furthermore, if your employer requests you take a preemployment drug test, he must be able to later prove (should you dispute this) that all employees in similar job classifications or types are tested.

If you are already employed, you could allege invasion of privacy when requested to submit to a drug test unless:

1. your employer has a written drug testing policy known to its employees, including an established grievance process should you refuse to be tested;
2. your employer can show that your insobriety/intoxication presents a danger to yourself and others;
3. your employer ensures that the results of the test are confidentially maintained; and
4. any "positive" result is independently confirmed.

In the event you refuse but are forced to submit to a drug test or have your blood extracted, you could have a potential case of assault and battery against your employer.

62. NO AIDS TESTING. PERIOD.

A 1987 Supreme Court decision listed three factors that can be used to determine whether a person can be refused a job or terminated because of any contagious disease (AIDS included), and they are:

1. the nature of the risk, its length and time, and risk severity;
2. the potential harm it (the disease) could impose on others; and
3. the possibility that it could be transmitted.

Since AIDS cannot be transmitted at work, it fails the the 3rd factor test as stated by the 1987 Supreme Court decision. This means that an employer cannot test you for AIDS. The ADA (Americans with Disabilities Act) also includes AIDS victims as "qualified disabled individuals" under its protection. Most states also specify that AIDS is a protected disability, and even in the minority of states that don't, an AIDS victim will certainly be protected by his or her state's civil rights or fair employment practices (FEP) laws.

63. BEWARE THE INDIRECT INTERVIEW QUESTIONS

"When I Asked If You Were Flexible, Mrs. Harkness, I Was Talking About Your Hours!

If there is one time where one can perhaps share a tinge of sympathy for the limitations heaped on the employer, it probably is during the preemployment or interview stage. Employers today are faced with a host of restrictions where it comes to interviewing you or administering preemployment questionnaires.

For example, in addition to the obvious potentially discriminatory questions about your age, sex, color, religion, ethnicity, and sexual orientation, an employer cannot pose indirect questions that could lead to a discriminatory employment decision. Some examples of forbidden preemployment questions include asking about:

1. your marital status;
2. whether you live with a member of the opposite sex (may indicate your sexual orientation);
3. whether you rent or own your residence (may indicate whether you are married);
4. when you graduated from college (may indicate your age);
5. whether you are pregnant or plan to have a family;
6. what religious holidays you observe;
7. whether you've been arrested for a crime (arrests don't count, only convictions); and
8. your height and/or weight.

Your employer cannot also ask you for a photo during the job application phase, as this could be used to discriminate against you on the basis of your race, color, ethnicity, sex, or age.

64. SHOULD YOU USE AN EMPLOYMENT AGENCY?

Deciding whether and when to use an employment agency is a matter of personal choice. But if you do decide to, consider this:

1. Know that there are laws requiring employment agencies to be licensed with your state department of labor. So check first with your state DOL to see if the agency you are dealing with is registered.
2. There are laws regulating what amount an employment agency can charge you—and also to inform you upfront what those fees are. You are also entitled to a partial refund if you don't remain on the job for a minimum period.
3. Employment agencies are subject to discrimination laws the same way employers are. They therefore cannot discriminate on the basis of age, sex, race, color, religion, marital status, etc.

The most important question you should ask your state DOL with regard to the employment agency is who pays the fee for making the referral to the employer—the employer or you.

65. WHY DON'T YOU NEGOTIATE YOUR CONTRACT?

Instead of just being grateful you got the job and consequently willing to sign anything in exchange for that regular wage, think the other way. Your employer wants you, too—it wouldn't otherwise be offering you the job. This is probably the only point in the employment relationship where you have some bargaining leverage. Other than negotiating your salary, use this opportunity to clarify that you want assurance that you can only be terminated after a fair process. Insist on clauses like automatic confirmation at the end of your probation period and an opportunity to be heard before firing, including termination only after a disciplinary procedure has been undertaken. Include, if you can, the requirement for "just cause." Terms like "fair," "justice," "just cause," and "equity" are all positively neutral-sounding words which you can use to your advantage. After all, almost everyone wants to be seen as fair and just, and the beginning of the relationship is the only time you can use this leverage to negotiate your terms.

66. AN ARREST IS NOT A CONVICTION

An arrest is not a conviction and cannot be treated as such by your employer. In the U.S. justice system, an individual is innocent until proven guilty. Your employer is therefore prohibited from making a hiring decision based on a prospective employee's past history. If you find yourself discriminated against based on your arrest record, you could sue on grounds of "adverse impact," especially if you can connect it to your race.

67. FALSE REPRESENTATION WORKS BOTH WAYS—YOU TOO CAN SUE

Much has been said about employees lying about their qualifications and experiences when applying for jobs. What about situations where the employer creates an illusory promise of job security to the employee by falsely positioning its organizational capacity and financial ability? In a landmark case of *Lazar Vs Rykoff-Sexton, Inc.*, the court found that Rykoff, a restaurant supply and equipment firm, had falsely represented itself when it offered the employee (Lazar) a job. The court found that Rykoff's description of itself as a fast-growing business operation with vast opportunities for career growth and succession had created a false perception in Lazar of job security and future career progression, which led him to relocate his family when accepting the job offer. When Lazar was terminated two years later on grounds of cost-cutting due to business losses, the court found that Rykoff had falsely represented itself to Lazar and awarded him compensation.

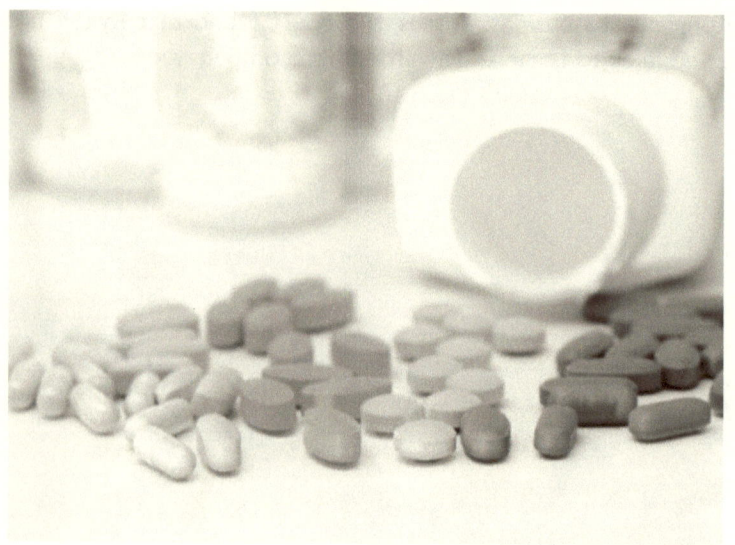

Medical & Disability

68. THE HEALTH CARE BILL

(I) How it Affects Your Employer's Insurance Plan

The statistics show that 60 percent of Americans buy insurance via their employer's private insurance plan. The long and short of the impact the 2010 health care law will have on these employees is that it will make it a little bit harder for a small number of "high-income" Americans while helping the rest or majority of us.

If you're an individual earning more than $200,000 or a family earning more than $250,000, your health care premiums are set to rise. You will be required to pay 2.35 percent Medicare payroll tax (up from 1.45 percent) on your earnings exceeding the $200,000/$250,000 threshold, plus a 3.8 percent Medicare payroll tax on any "unearned" income.

Also, for those of you enrolled in expensive employer insurance (about 19 percent of the workforce), the government, starting in 2018, will levy a 40 percent surtax on insurers that offer plans costing $10,200 per year for individuals and $27,500 for families. Typically, these expensive plans don't require co-payments or deductibles for doctors or hospital visits—giving enrollees little reason to economize. The rationale behind this surtax is to force "premium" consumers to be more price conscious and opt for cheaper plans.

The vast majority of Americans who buy insurance through their employers will not experience higher health care costs or interruptions in their coverage. On the contrary, it will probably improve. If you are a family of four with two parents earning a combined annual income of $110,000 and purchase "moderately" priced insurance, you will almost certainly be better off. Your insurer will, for instance, no longer be able to place a lifetime dollar limit on their coverage or cancel your policy (unless there was evidence of fraud). Also, if you happen to lose your job, you'd still be able to buy reasonably priced insurance even if you have a pre-existing medical condition.

(II) What if Your Employer is a Small Business Owner?

If your employer has more than fifty full-time employees, the new health care bill mandates that he provide all his employers with insurance, failing which he will have to pay a fine of $750. Employers with fewer than fifty employees, while not required to provide insurance, get serious incentives to provide insurance coverage. If your employer employs ten people, for example, and only pays half your insurance premiums, the government steps in with another 35 percent, while all you need to pay is the balance, 15 percent. This tax credit to employers will grow from 35 percent to 50 percent in 2014.

(III) What if I Have a Preexisting Medical Condition?

The biggest innovation of the health care law is the creation of health insurance exchanges as a principal tool in expanding coverage and containing health care costs. Here, each state will have a virtual marketplace where individuals and those working in small businesses can "pool" or group their purchasing power and shop for plans.

When these exchanges come into force in 2014, insurers will be prohibited from rejecting customers or charging higher rates for their preexisting medical condition. What happens if you are suffering from a preexisting medical condition now?

The answer for you lies in a "high risk pool" created under the bill that provides for a cap on your premiums and out-of-pocket spending—with the government subsidizing the rest. There is a catch, however! You can only qualify for this "high risk pool" provided you have been without coverage for at least six months. The reason behind this is to stop people from switching from their private insurance plan to this government-subsidized plan.

(IV) How the Health Care Bill Helps You if You're Under Twenty-six

Under new rules that kicked in late in 2010, insurance companies have to extend coverage to all dependents younger than twenty-six years of age (before that, coverage lapsed upon completion of high school). If you can't rely on your parents' coverage, you must find your own coverage or pay a fine of $95. Bear in mind that this fine will increase to $325 in 2015 and $695 in 2016. If you are, however, unable to find affordable coverage—defined as less than 8 percent of your income—you are exempt.

(V) How the Bill Protects Low-earning Americans

Low-earning Americans are defined as those earning less than 150 percent of the Federal Poverty Line (FPL). For individuals, this amount is $16,425 annually. If you are a family of four earning between 133 percent and 150 percent of the FPL (between $29,000 and $33,000), your health insurance premiums will be capped at 4 percent of your income—and the government picks up the rest of the tab. Any out-of-pocket expenses you incur will additionally be capped at 15 percent of your income. In addition, by January 1, 2014, any American earning less than $14,400 (or 133 percent of the FPL) will be automatically eligible for Medicaid.

(VI) No Subsidizing Abortions

Under this bill, the government will not subsidize any abortions. This in effect will mean that when the new insurance exchange is set up, two schemes will be offered—one providing coverage for possible abortions and another for everything else. As separating the coverage under two headings will likely cost insurers administratively, pro-choice advocates worry that this will lead them to stop offering coverage—meaning that the 1.2 million Americans that undergo abortions yearly may be faced with no choice but to pay for them out of their own pockets!

69. YOU STILL HAVE RIGHTS TO BE COMPENSATED EVEN WITH A PREEXISTING ILLNESS

Workers' compensation insurance costs employers. As their premium rates depend on the number of claims made by employees, employers naturally want to minimize their exposure here. So what happens if you have a preexisting injury (let's say you've had knee surgery) and your prospective employer fears hiring you on grounds that there's a likelihood you may later file a workers' compensation claim?

Well, if your prospective employer brings this up (better yet, take the initiative and inform him yourself), tell him that you are willing to sign a waiver in case of reinjury. Don't worry, because if you sustain the same injury, you've not lost your entitlement despite signing the waiver. You are still covered, and what happens is that your benefits will come from a state "second injury fund" which will not come from your employer. So, you've nothing to lose by signing this waiver (for reinjury).

70. DEPRESSION IS A DISABILITY, AND SO IS DIABETES

For The Last Time Our Son Is Not Backwards. He's Just Dyslexic

The Americans with Disabilities Act or ADA is the law that protects people/employees with disabilities. The courts have ruled that in determining whether a person's illness is a "protected disability," the test applied is not the diagnosis per se but the impact of the illness on the person's ability to perform the job. It is for this reason that depression and emotional illnesses are qualified as protected disabilities.

On September 25, 2008, President George W. Bush signed the Americans with Disabilities Act Amendments Act of 2008. These amendments have basically emphasized that the definition of a disability should be construed in a "broad" context. These amendments have in effect rejected several of the Supreme Court decisions and portions of the EEOC's ADA regulations, making it easier for an individual to claim that he or she has a disability.

As a result of these amendments, illnesses such as diabetes or epilepsy that were earlier classified as impairments that were episodic or can be controllable by medications—and henceforth not disabilities under the act—now qualify! So too does carpal tunnel syndrome if you're able to demonstrate that it affects your ability to perform your work.

71. HERE'S WHAT YOU DO IF YOU HAVE A DISABILITY

If you have a protected disability, don't assume that the ADA requires your employer to made "accommodations" for your disability. Rather, it is up to you to suggest the accommodations you require. In suggesting the accommodations:

1. analyze the essential functions of the job and list what limitations your disability imposes on your ability to perform the function;
2. identify the accommodations you require and how each of them will aid you in effectively performing your work functions; and
3. list the availability and costs of the accommodations, including how long each will be required.

Remember, the onus is on you to suggest the accommodation.

72. WHAT TO TELL YOUR PROSPECTIVE EMPLOYER IF YOU'RE TOLD YOUR DISABILITY COSTS HIM TOO MUCH

To show that it cannot make any accommodations for your disability, your employer will have to prove "undue hardship", i.e., that he can't afford them. This is not easy for the employer, as he would have to justify to the EEOC that he doesn't have the financial resources to do so. Furthermore, many accommodations, such as raising/reducing the work station height levels or providing ergonomic chairs, aren't costly. The bigger the organization (be it in terms of the employee size or revenue), the less likely it'll be able to get away with pleading undue hardship, particularly with the tax deductions it can claim for making the accommodation.

73. YOU HAVE A RIGHT TO CLAIM BOTH WORKERS' COMPENSATION AND SOCIAL SECURITY DISABILITY INSURANCE

The law provides you with the option of claiming income from both workers' compensation and Social Security. The only requirement is that the combined benefits offered by both cannot exceed 80 percent of your average wages prior to your disablement.

74. YOUR COBRA RIGHTS

Health insurance is an expensive proposition, particularly when you are recently unemployed. This is where the Consolidated Omnibus Budget Reconciliation Act, or COBRA, helps you. COBRA requires that your employer (upon your termination/resignation) provide you with the option of continuing your coverage under the company's group health insurance plan for at least eighteen months. The catch here is that you have to pay the employer's part of the premiums yourself, although it may be cheaper continuing your coverage under the group health plan than having to fork out for an individual plan.

75. MAKE COBRA WORK FOR YOU

COBRA essentially covers you and your spouse/dependent's rights to continue with your company group medical insurance coverage (which may be cheaper than getting an individual policy) in the event of a qualifying event, such as your termination from employment, or death.

In the event you resign or are terminated (for reasons other than a gross misconduct), COBRA entitles you and your spouse/dependents to be given the right by your employer to continue with the company's group medical insurance coverage. If you are divorced or die, your spouse and dependents are provided with this coverage option for up to thirty-six months.

Termination
and Leaving

76. DON'T GO FOR THE EXIT INTERVIEW

You have nothing to gain from an exit interview, other than to collect your paycheck (which you can collect by other means, like asking the company to mail it, direct deposit it, etc). Your employer cannot force you to attend an exit interview as a precondition for getting your paycheck.

Attorneys will typically advise employers to get employees to sign a waiver not to sue during the exit interview. So you may find yourself in a vulnerable situation where, already stunned and in disbelief by your shock firing, you are left sitting opposite your boss, who, together with someone from human resources, is rationalizing about how he's tried his best to keep your interests at heart in softening the blow. Then this is followed up with the presentation of the waiver for you to sign!!

77. KEEP A COPY OF YOUR DISCIPLINARY RECORDS

You should keep records of all or any disciplinary action taken against you, even the verbal or oral warnings. Your employer, after all, certainly keeps a record of them in your personnel files. The other reason for keeping your own records is that an unscrupulous employer may even be tempted to doctor/tamper with any disciplinary action (particularly if he knows he has a weak case).

Also, don't stop at just keeping a copy of the disciplinary letter. Actively keep your own detailed notes of the incident(s), including notes of any meeting(s) that took place between you and your boss.

The other thing you can do if you are given a disciplinary action you feel is unfair is to note your disagreement alongside your signature. You also have a right to request your employer keep your own detailed report of the incident in your records.

Finally, don't leave things till later. As soon as you come out of the disciplinary meeting, write down details of the incident, including what your superior said. There have been cases where an employee used his superior's assurance that the disciplinary action was merely "company-required procedure" and that "he had nothing to worry about" in court to prove that his subsequent dismissal had been unfair.

78. START EARLY AND DOCUMENT EVERYTHING

When you start your first day on the job, all may be hunky dory. You may even have visions of how you are going to be the toast of the office, winning over colleagues, impressing the bosses, and in no time rising up the corporate ladder, earning loads of bucks. This rose-colored vision of the world provides indeed a wonderful stimulation for the future expectation of glory. Only one problem: it seldom happens. The reality of corporate life is that people have their own agendas, and, unfortunately, some will stoop to undermining and diminishing your credibility to get ahead.

Stay ahead of the game here and see reality as opposed to fiction. You may be one of the few fortunate souls that have a blessed employer that knows how to promote an internal win-win corporate culture, but these employers are in the minority. So how do you stay ahead insofar as your rights at work are concerned?

One word: document. Do this early, and document everything from the job advertisement, your job application form, any aptitude and preemployment tests you took, the company's handbook (including any changes with the date of change), your performance reviews, memos and disciplinary documents issued to you, your termination notices, as well as your own personal report of incidents.

Finally, employers sometimes have informal meetings or pep talks where they may discuss new rules or policies without ever putting them into writing. Document your own record of what transpired, what was said by whom, and other details, such as the date, time, and place.

You may not necessarily decide to sue, but by keeping a record of all that has taken place, you're in the driver's seat when it comes to deciding whether legal action is needed. And as the saying goes in law, "The party with the thickest load of documents usually wins in court..."

79. HAVE I BEEN FAIRLY DISCHARGED? YOUR OWN CHECKLIST

If you've been discharged or dismissed, use this checklist to determine whether you have a case against your employer:

1. Was I in any way discriminated against, be it on grounds of sex, age, religion, race, color, or ethnicity?
2. Were any FLSA rights violated, such as my minimum wage, overtime, and hours of work?
3. Did the employer violate any of my privacy rights, i.e., my confidentiality rights to personal property, medical records, past employment history, etc.?
4. Where terminated on grounds of "business necessity," was I terminated because I was a member of a "protected group"?
5. Was my termination done diligently with due process, or did my employer hastily, irrationally terminate my services?
6. Where terminated on grounds of performance, did my employer's actions contradict my recent performance reviews?
7. Was my termination linked to my having reported OSHA violations, accounting violations, or my superior for unethical behavior?
8. Did my employer try to get me to sign a waiver? Remember, a waiver is meaningless if you can prove it was coerced or fraudulently obtained.

80. HOW TO FIGHT A DEFAMATORY JOB REFERENCE

There are defamation laws that protect you, including laws against a former employer providing your prospective employer with negative information about you. Lockheed Corporation found this out the hard way when a California jury awarded its former employee almost a cool $1 million after finding that Lockheed had provided his prospective employers with a defamatory job reference, which the court agreed had caused him to suffer emotional stress.

In addition to defamation, there are also blackmailing laws that protect you. You've probably seen this on TV where the swaggering boss with an exaggerated sense of self-importance confronts the meek, subservient staff and says, "You're finished. You're never gonna get a job in this industry as long as I'm living!"

Well, if this happens to you, document it. If you are able to show proof that this employer has, in fact, circulated your name to the industry with the intent of preventing you from obtaining future employment, you'll likely win.

81. YOU MAY HAVE AN "IMPLIED CONTRACT"

Imagine this scenario. You sign an employment contract stipulating that the employment relationship is on an "at will" basis—which means your employer can fire you without any reason. Three months into the job, your boss calls you in, commends you on your performance, and assures you that you have a job for life as long as you keep up the good work.

Two months later, you're handed a termination notice (despite continuing to perform) which points to the "employment at will" clause you signed acceptance to in your employment contract.

Do you have recourse?

The answer is yes if you can prove that by promising you job security as long as you performed, your employer had created an "implied contract." To prove this, ensure that you documented the date, time, and place the oral assurance was made, including what was actually said. Another strategy you could undertake is, upon receiving the termination letter, to write to your employer and remind him of the oral assurance that was given to you (provide details). Then ask him to confirm that this took place, failing which you will have no choice but to contend that your employer had created an "implied contract" which he violated.

The essence behind you sending this letter is to build up your case for future legal action.

82. HOW TO OBTAIN A JOB REFERENCE WHEN YOU LEAVE A STICKY JOB SITUATION

If you part with your organization on unhappy terms, there is a stronger likelihood that it may not give you the glowing recommendation you wish for. Far from that, it is likely not going to contain anything positive.

Instead of losing sleep over what your past employer may say, seize the initiative by asking him for a job reference then and there, when you leave the job. As your employer is unlikely willing to take the risk of providing you with a negative job reference (for fear of legal action), you head off this possibility by obtaining a neutral reference. Sure, the job reference you obtain may likely only state particulars such as your name, rank, and length of service, but at least you have a neutral reference in your hand which you can use for future job-hunting purposes.

83. USE THE EMPLOYEE HANDBOOK TO YOUR ADVANTAGE

An employee handbook typically contains statements on the company's rules, regulations, policies, and procedures, as well as disciplinary processes. Some companies don't have employee handbooks, and without them the only document an employer can then rely on will typically be the employment contract.

If your employer has an employee handbook, look out for the following:

1. Does he have a disciplinary process in place for managing performance and misconducts? If a process is stated but not adhered to when terminating the employee, the employee could claim unfair discharge (despite the employer having an at-will policy).
2. Does the handbook state that employees can only be fired for "just cause"? If so, it supersedes any stipulated employment-at-will policy.

3. Does the handbook contain a promise for a hearing before dismissal? If so, the employer must give the employee an opportunity to be heard before firing.

4. Does the handbook state that following a probation period, the employee will be considered as "full time" or "permanent"? While the term "full time" is noncontradictory, stating that an employee is categorized as "permanent" means that he/she now has a lien on the job, so to speak—which could be deemed a contradiction or in conflict with any at-will clause.

The key, therefore, is to read your employee handbook thoroughly. Go through it with a fine-tooth comb, particularly the aspects governing at will, just cause, and disciplinary procedures. You may just find a passage or two in your favor.

84. ASK FOR THE REASONS FOR YOUR TERMINATION (IN WRITING)

You have a right to request for a written statement explaining the reasons for your termination. To induce your employer to provide this written explanation, write to him yourself first and make it clear to him that without knowing the reasons behind your termination, you have no option other than to contend you've been discriminated against and will persue legal remedies. This usually will provide your employer with the impetus to provide you with a written explanation.

85. YOUR EMPLOYER STILL REFUSES TO PROVIDE YOU WITH A WRITTEN EXPLANATION? TRY THIS.

If you find your request for a written explanation for your termination is not met with a response, it's time to change gears and adopt a different tack. Try writing again to your employer, only this time, in no-nonsense, objective language, state matter-of-factly what you believe are the real reasons for your termination. You could say, for instance:

"I believe I was fired due to your disappointment with me raising a complaint on the factory's safety standards," or "I believe I was dismissed due to reasons related to my race."

Then, in this same letter, inform the employer that you hope to receive his response within a certain time frame, failing which you will assume that the reasons you stated in your letter were the factors behind your dismissal/termination.

86. WALK OUT—DON'T WAIT AND SUFFER
(CONSTRUCTIVE DISCHARGE)

If you find that you are being sexually harassed, you should lodge a complaint within your organization using its grievance process. What happens, however, if your complaint is met with nonaction?

Well, in this circumstance, the law helps you by allowing you to walk out on your employer by claiming "constructive discharge."

Constructive discharge happens when an employee walks out on the employer on grounds that the employer's actions or nonactions have made the employment relationship intolerable. In effect, the employee is essentially stating that the employer has made it virtually impossible for him/her to continue on the job.

Sexual harassment isn't the only circumstance entitling an employee to claim constructive discharge. An employee placed on "cold storage" for reporting a safety violation could also, for instance, walk out if he/she can prove that by taking away his/her job functions, the employer has created an intolerable employment situation.

87. AFTER PROBATION, YOU COULD BE DEEMED PERMANENT

Your employer may unwittingly have shot itself in the foot if it states either orally or in writing that once you have successfully completed your probation, you will be deemed a "permanent" employee. By stating you are permanent, you could now argue that this means you have superior rights to an employee "at will" and that, in order to dismiss you, your employer must have just cause.

Similarly, if your employer labels you as a full-time employee upon confirmation, you could argue that you are now entitled to a full forty-hour workweek, and any decision later undertaken to shift you back as a part-time employee is a breach of the employment contract.

88. NONCOMPETE CLAUSE—YOU CAN FIND LOOPHOLES

Employers have the right to require employees to sign an agreement "not to compete" provided that the terms of the agreement are reasonable with regard to its scope, time period, and geographical area. For instance, your employer has the right to stipulate in its noncompete agreement that you cannot, upon leaving the organization, join specific competitors in a similar capacity for a certain time frame. It cannot, however, word its noncompete clause in general terms, such as prohibiting you from working with any organization within the industry nationwide for five years. The enforceability of a noncompete clause rests primarily on whether it is reasonable (i.e., it is required to protect your employer's legitimate business interest) and is specific (in terms of its scope, time frame, and geographical area).

Another thing to consider is that even if you sign a noncompete clause but later join another employer within the industry, your ex-employer, in enforcing the noncompete agreement, will have to prove that the clause was legitimately required and reasonable. If it can't prove this to the court's satisfaction, then the courts simply won't enforce it.

89. EMPLOYMENT "AT WILL" VERSUS CIVIL RIGHTS VIOLATIONS—KNOW WHEN EACH APPLIES

In raising a complaint, you will need to first identify if the nature of the allegation involves a Title VII civil rights violation or if it concerns your employer wrongfully exercising its employment-at-will right to fire you.

Know that you have only three grounds in challenging your employer's right to terminate using employment at will. The first is that via actions such as giving you verbal assurances of your job security, your employer has, in effect, created an "implied promise" that you cannot be terminated using employment at will. The second ground is "just cause," where you could allege that, via past practice with other employees in similar situations where your employer first invoked a disciplinary process, it had created an expectation that you can only be terminated with or after a disciplinary process has been instituted against you. The third ground you could use is where you employer's actions of terminating your services violates a federal or state law or city ordinance. An example of public policy violations is where you are fired for reporting a safety violation to the Occupational Safety and Health authorities.

A civil rights violation, on the other hand, occurs when you have been terminated on grounds that you believe are related to your age, sex, color, race, ethnicity, disability, military status, sexual orientation, or marital status.

Naturally, sometimes your termination could be linked to both. For example, your employer could exercise its right to terminate your services at will, but you know that the real reason the at-will clause was used in the first place was due to your race!

90. YOU MAY ALSO BE ENTITLED TO FRONT PAY

"Front pay" refers to compensation you stand to earn if the court finds that giving you back your job isn't practical under the circumstances. The reasons for not giving you back your job could be that the court finds that your relationship with your employer has irretrievably broken down or that there is no longer a position for you in the organization. In such a situation, the court can, in addition to awarding you back pay, add another compensation element called front pay, which is essentially the pay you would have earned had you been reinstated!

91. HOW MUCH MONEY CAN I WIN—CIVIL RIGHTS VIOLATIONS

For any civil rights violation proven in court, you stand to earn:

1. back pay, which refers to the money you would have earned had you not been terminated (till the award date);
2. front pay if the court finds that putting you back in your old job is no longer tenable;
3. damages of up to $300,000, depending on the staffing size of your employer; and
4. attorney fees and court costs.

92. SUE UNDER STATE LAW, NOT FEDERAL LAW

Suing your employer under federal law implies, for some, a grander, bigger payout, as the assumption here is we are taking our legal rights national. The opposite, however, is true, particularly with regard to civil rights violations. State cases are not only usually easier to win, but they also have a higher possibility for your employer's winning a larger award judgment due to the fact that state laws are usually more supportive and protective of employee rights.

93. YOU MAY STILL KEEP YOUR SEVERANCE PAY DESPITE SIGNING AN ADEA WAIVER

ADEA refers to the Age Discrimination in Employment Act, which essentially protects you if you are forty years or older. Employers sometimes try

74

to overcome ADEA restrictions by getting their employees to sign waivers or an agreement not to sue in exchange for a severance package. While the law does permit an employer and employee to negotiate a waiver, it contains several restrictions, including requiring:

1. that the severance package is higher or superior to the law or company policy;
2. that it gives the employee at least twenty-one days to decide if he/she wants to sign the waiver (forty-five days if presented to a group);
3. that, when presented to a group of employees, it specifies how each class/group of employees is identified, including the job titles and ages of all those offered the severance;
4. that it must specify the employee's right to consult an attorney; and
5. that it covers all the employee's ADEA rights and is made understandable to him/her.

If the criteria above are not met, the waiver the employee signed is "deficient"—meaning that the employee can still sue for age discrimination and *keep the severance pay earlier received!*

94. YOUR UNION'S COLLECTIVE AGREEMENT MAY HAVE A "JUST CAUSE" CLAUSE

If you belong to a union, be sure to read the collective agreement signed between your employer and union. It may very well contain a clause stating that unionized employees can only be terminated with just cause, meaning that your employer is prohibited from applying employment at will when choosing to fire its unionized employees.

95. THE AGREEMENT NOT TO SUE THAT YOU SIGNED MAY NOT BE VALID

It's o.k he has signed-release his children

Visualize this scene: A member of the company's human resources department, together with your superior, walks into your work station and bluntly informs you that you're fired. You're then asked to sign a waiver (an agreement not to sue) and told that if you agree, a further three-months' severance pay will be given to you. You're also told that if you don't sign it, you'll get nothing. As you're told this, the human resource member holds up an envelope indicating your check is in it. Stunned, embarrassed, confused, you sign the waiver, take the check, clean your station, and are escorted out.

It is now one week later. You've recovered from the shock and regained some of your composure. However, while you're upset, you feel there's nothing you can do as you had signed that waiver.

Well, the good news is you may still have a case. If you can prove that the waiver was obtained under coercion or duress, the courts could yet rule that the waiver you signed isn't valid, entitling you to proceed with your unfair discharge claim.

96. KNOW WHAT WARN MEANS

WARN refers to the Workers' Adjustment and Retraining Notification Act, which governs plant closings. Generally, it requires that an employer with one hundred or more full-time employees must give its employees at least sixty days' advance, written notice that they are about to lose their jobs before a plant closing.

97. KNOW YOUR RIGHTS TO REPLACEMENT INCOME WHEN YOU LOSE YOUR JOB

There are three types of income replacement programs that you are/may be eligible for when you've lost your job. The first is unemployment insurance when you lose your job through no fault of your own, such as a company closing or retrenchment. The second is workers' compensation insurance, which pays for your medical bills for injuries/illnesses you sustain at work, including compensating you for permanent injuries. Your loved ones are also entitled to compensation from this provision if you die from a workplace injury/illness.

The third is Social Security disability income, which provides you with income in the event you can't work for at least twelve months due to an injury or illness. Social Security disability income covers you whether or not the injury/illness sustained occurred at work.

98. YOU DON'T NEED TO BE ON WELFARE TO RECEIVE FOOD STAMPS

Food stamps are, in actuality, financed by the U.S. Department of Labor as a means for increasing demand for food products. They are not a form of welfare!

If you find that your income has been reduced significantly or is now non-existent, you could very well qualify for food stamp assistance. Enquire within your local office of the U.S. Department of Agriculture on your eligibility for them.

99. YOU MAY BE ELIGIBLE FOR SOCIAL SECURITY DESPITE NEVER CONTRIBUTING IN THE PAST

There is another little-known provision called Supplementary Security Income, or SSI, which you can be eligible for despite never contributing to Social Security in the past. Contact your local Social Security Administration office about your rights under SSI.

100. YOU COULD STILL QUALIFY FOR UNEMPLOYMENT INSURANCE DESPITE QUITTING YOUR JOB

An employee is usually entitled to unemployment insurance when he/she is fired from the job. However, you could walk out and claim "constructive discharge" in situations where you feel your employer's conduct has made it virtually impossible for you to continue working. In order to be entitled to unemployment insurance when claiming constructive discharge, the employee must be able to naturally prove his/her claim.

Some valid reasons for claiming constructive discharge that have held up in the past include:

1. when an employee reports a sexual harassment incident which is ignored by the employer;

2. when an employee walks out on grounds that his/her health and safety are compromised due to hazardous/dangerous working conditions;
3. when an employer promises certain benefits/entitlements which the employee finds to be nonexistent; or
4. when the nature of the employee's function or job changes dramatically from what he/she was hired to do.

101. UNDERSTAND YOUR ERISA RIGHTS

ERISA is the acronym that stands for the Employee Retirement Income Security Act. The primary purpose of ERISA is to protect employees (and their beneficiaries) who participate in employee benefit plans. ERISA, however, only applies to private employers and does not mandate that an employer must offer you a pension plan. It does, however, require that once your employer chooses to offer you a pension plan, it must meet minimum standards in protecting employees and their beneficiaries. Some important protective elements of ERISA include:

1. requiring that employees be provided with details of any pension plans provided, including a summary plan description, what it provides, how it operates, how service and benefits are calculated, when benefits become vested, when and in what form benefits are paid, and how to file a claim for benefits;
2. requiring that the plan administrator provides participants with a copy of the plan's summary and annual financial report; and
3. ensuring that fiduciaries running the plan(s) do so solely with the best interests of the participants and their beneficiaries.

102. BANKRUPTCY OF YOUR EMPLOYER— WHAT HAPPENS TO YOUR PENSION

'Not scared yet? Just wait until I get to Chapter 11!"

ERISA, the Employee Retirement Income Security Act, regulates most private-sector pension plans and employee benefit plans, such as health insurance, life insurance, disability, severance, etc. Designed to protect employees from abuses in the administration of private-sector benefit plans, ERISA also created the Pension Benefit Guaranty Corporation (PBGC), which insures benefits under defined benefit pension plans. Where insolvency occurs, PBGC takes over the pension plan and pays out retiree benefits although it probably will be less than what is provided in the original plan.

The PBGC maximum per-person benefits are limited to $54,000 per year for someone retiring at the normal retirement age of sixty-five. For airline pilots who are required to retire at sixty, the maximum benefit is even lower, as it is considered as early retirement under PBGC.

Some Important Court Decisions You Oughta Be Aware Of

CASE I

Your employer can get into trouble for luring you to join the organization under false pretenses.

Case Featured:

Lazar v. Superior Court
California Supreme Court No S044186 (1996)

INTRODUCTION

Lazar, a New York native, was happily working for a family-owned restaurant there earning an annual salary of $120,000. He was then approached by Rykoff-Sexton, Inc., to come and work as its West Coast general manager for contract design in Los Angeles. In attracting Lazar, Rykoff painted a picture that it was financially stable with strong opportunities for advancement. Rykoff also intimated to Lazar that the department he would be working in represented a growth division of the company.

Lazar accepted appointment with Rykoff based on these assurances. He uprooted his family (wife and two kids) to Los Angeles, bought a home, and commenced work with a starting salary of $130,000. He soon started contributing, helping his department reduce its operating budget and increase sales.

Some two years into his employment, Lazar was surprised to be told that his position was being eliminated due to management reorganization. He was then informed that if he chose to instead resign, Rykoff would allow him to keep his job for three months, giving him time to search for a new job. However, word of Lazar leaving Rykoff was not kept a secret and became common knowledge within the industry, rendering him unable to find comparable employment.

This led Lazar to sue Rykoff on the grounds that it had misrepresented itself in luring him to join the organization. He further alleged that since Rykoff was aware that it was not financially stable when it offered him the position, its misrepresentation amounted to a fraudulent misrepresentation. Both the state district and appeals court, however, found no such evidence of fraudulent inducement, leaving Lazar to appeal this decision at the state supreme court.

WHAT THE COURT DECIDED

The California Supreme Court held in favor of Lazar, finding that Rykoff had been guilty of "fraudulently inducing" him to enter into an employment relationship. In finding that Rykoff's actions amounted to a breach of contract and fraud, it also awarded tort damages to Lazard.

In its ruling that Lazar had been fraudulently induced, the Court stated the following:

"As to his fraud claim Lazar may properly seek damages for the costs of uprooting his family, expenses incurred in relocation, and the loss of security and income associated with his former employment in New York. Lazar, therefore, may proceed with his claim for fraud in the inducement of employment contract, properly seeking damages for 'all the detriment proximately caused thereby,' <u>as well as appropriate exemplary damages</u>."

Note: A tort action arises when one party pursues civil action against another for damages or injuries (physical and emotional) suffered. If the suing party is successful, he/she would, in addition to any contractual damages payable under the law, be entitled to compensation for any emotional or physical injuries suffered, including punitive damages.

HOW YOU CAN BENEFIT FROM THIS CASE

1. KNOW THE CIRCUMSTANCES (WHERE YOU CAN ALLEGE MISREPRESENTATION/FRAUDULENT INDUCEMENT)

Don't go rushing to a lawyer thinking that any semblance of a wrongful promise or inducement of any sort by your supervisor constitutes a misrepresentation or fraudulent inducement. To be successful in any claim, you'll need to show how you've suffered or been wronged as a result of this misrepresentation. This means that your recourse usually only begins when you have been fired, as it is typically then that you find yourself without a job or future employment prospects.

2. BEWARE OF AN EMPLOYER'S RESIGNATION PLOY

As with Lazar's case, some employers may be deceptive and try to obtain an employee's resignation instead of firing them. This is usually done in situations where:

1. the employer knows that terminating the employee outright could lead to a lawsuit; or
2. terminating the employee's services without due process is against company policy.

If you're faced with such a situation, you could have a valid action for fraud against your manager and employer. See what the court in Lazar's case stated below in regard to this issue of induced resignations:

"Under some circumstances, the employer will refrain from discharging the employee outright because it is too costly to do so. Employers may, for example, resort to such fraudulent deception when they know that to terminate the employee straightforwardly will lead to a lawsuit in which the employee would likely prevail. This species of fraud may

be especially common in those situations in which a manager superior to the employee seeks to be rid of the employee, but finds such a decision to be at variance with official company policy. In such a case, the manager may seek not only to avoid potential lawsuits, but also the employer's internal disciplinary processes by obtaining the employee's resignation through trickery. Under those circumstances, the employee would likely not have been fired unless the manager could resort to deception. Therefore the employee who resigns in reliance on such deception can be said to have 'detrimentally relied,' by any reasonable understanding of that term. The employee would therefore have a <u>cognizable action for fraud</u> against the manager and against his employer."

3. AGGRESSIVE RECRUITMENT STRATEGIES – HAVE YOU BEEN FRAUDULENTLY INDUCED?

During the dot-com bubble of 2000–2001, many companies, in response to the then ultracompetitive business environment, adopted aggressive recruiting strategies to attract talent. Promises were made concerning funding levels, merger prospects, and product development in attracting talent. During this period, it was estimated that between one third and two thirds of wrongful termination complaints filed were by employees alleging fraudulent inducement. Most stemmed from allegations they were misled into signing employment contracts by their employer on promises of stable business prospects and the company going public in the near future.

If you today are faced with a similar situation and are uncertain about your employer's prospects, take down notes of all promises (be they oral or in writing) and keep copies of any letters/documentation received. You never know—you may just need them later when you find yourself without a job!

CASE 2

Your employer can be held liable for any sexual harassment you encounter at work.

Case Featured

Faragher v. City of Boca Raton
(The United States Supreme Court)
Case No 97-282 (1998)

INTRODUCTION

Beth Ann Faragher worked part time during the summer for the City of Boca Raton as an ocean lifeguard attached with its Marine Safety Section of the Parks and Recreation Department. She reported to three immediate superiors, namely Bill Terry, David Silverman, and Robert Gordon. She resigned after spending five years there and brought an action against two of her supervisors, namely Bill Terry and David Silverman, and the city under Title VII of the Civil Rights Act for sexual harassment.

Faragher alleged that both Terry and Silverman had created a sexually hostile work atmosphere at the beach by repeatedly subjecting her (and other female lifeguards) to uninvited and offensive touching, making lewd remarks, and, in general, speaking of women in degrading terms. She also claimed that Terry had told her that he would never promote a woman to the rank of lieutenant, and that Silverman had said to her "date me or clean the toilets for a year." She further asserted that as Terry and Silverman were employees of the city, the city should be held vicariously liable for their actions.

Her employer, the City of Boca Raton, did initiate an investigation into Faragher's complaint. However, upon finding that Terry and Silverman had behaved improperly, the city merely chose to reprimand them while giving them the option of choosing a suspension without pay or a forfeiture of their annual leave.

Disillusioned with the city's level of punishment, Faragher sued the city. The district court found in Faragher's favor, holding that since the city had knowledge of the harassment, it was liable under traditional agency principles as Terry and Silverman were acting as its agents when committing the harassment act. The state court of appeal, however, reversed this decision, leading to Faragher bringing this matter before the state supreme court.

WHAT THE COURT DECIDED

The Supreme Court of the United States held in favor of Faragher, ruling that the City of Boca Raton was "vicariously liable" for the sexual harassment acts committed by its two supervisors, Terry and Silverman. In explaining its decision that employers can be held vicariously liable for the conduct of their supervisors, the Court stated the following:

"Recognition of employer liability when discriminatory misuse of supervisory authority alters the terms and conditions of a victim's employment is underscored by the fact that the employer has greater opportunity to guard against misconduct by supervisors than by common workers; employer have greater incentive to screen them, train them, and monitor their performance. In sum, there are good reasons for vicarious liability for misuse of supervisory authority."

HOW YOU CAN BENEFIT FROM THIS CASE

1. YOUR EMPLOYER CAN BE HELD VICARIOUSLY LIABLE

If you've been sexually harassed by your supervisor at work, you could sue your employer under the doctrine of vicarious liability. Vicarious liability in employment situations occurs when an employer is held accountable for actions (such as harassment) committed by its supervisors against employees. Hence, if you've been sexually harassed at work, you can sue both the person(s) harassing you as well as your employer.

2. BUT YOUR EMPLOYER CAN ALSO DEFEND ITSELF

While it's all good that you can hold your employer accountable for actions committed by its supervisors, fairness also dictates that an employer should be allowed to show evidence that it tried to stem the harassment from taking place, otherwise known as an affirmative defense. Affirmative defense in this context means that if an employer can demonstrate that it had taken actions to minimize or mitigate such behavior, it should not be held vicariously responsible for its supervisors' actions. Some examples of an affirmative defense include your employer demonstrating to the courts that it:

1. has a sexual harassment policy (which includes a clear complaint procedure) in place that was effectively communicated to all employees;
2. responded to any harassment allegation promptly and took the necessary preventive and remedial action; and
3. initiated steps to prevent further harm to the victimized employee.

Bear in mind, though, that if your employer has a sexual harassment policy but either did not communicate it effectively to employees nor take preventive action after a complaint was raised, it can still be held vicariously liable.

CASE 3

The definition of a 'qualifying disability' under the Americans with Disabilities Act, or ADA, has been greatly expanded.

Case Featured

Toyota Motor Manufacturing, Kentucky, Inc. v. Williams
(Kentucky Supreme Court)
Case No 00-189 (2002)

INTRODUCTION

Note: The significance of this case has been nullified by the amendments to the Americans with Disabilities Act (ADA) that were signed into law by former President Bush (they took effect beginning in 2009). You'll find the impact of these amendments discussed in the "how you can benefit from this case" section.

Due to the strain arising from performing repetitive manual tasks at Toyota's assembly line, Williams developed carpal tunnel syndrome. Due to this injury, Williams went on frequent leav,e which led to Toyota issuing her a termination letter. This led her to sue Toyota for failing to provide her with reasonable accommodation as required under the Americans with Disabilities Act.

The state district court, however, found in Toyota's favor by ruling that since Williams's injury did not substantially limit her from performing "major life functions" such as walking and bending, it could not be classified as a disability under the ADA. The state court of appeals, however, reversed the district court's decision, leading Toyota to appeal this decision before the state supreme court.

WHAT THE COURT HELD

The Kentucky Supreme Court held in Toyota's favor, effectively reversing the court of appeals' decision. In its decision that Williams's impairment did not meet the test of a "substantial limitation of a major life activity," the Court issued these two important quotes:

<u>On What Constitutes a Major Life Activity</u>

"Major" in the phrase major life activities means important. It refers to those activities that are of central importance to daily life. In order for manual tasks to fit into this category—a category that includes basic abilities such as walking, seeing and hearing—the manual task in question must be central to daily life. If each of the tasks included in the major life activity of performing manual tasks does not independently qualify as a major life activity, then together they must do.

HOW YOU CAN BENEFIT FROM THIS CASE

1. NEW AMENDMENTS HAVE EMERGED REVERSING THE TOYOTA CASE DECISION

On September 25, 2008, President Bush signed the ADA Amendment, which lowered the threshold test of what constitutes a "major life function" and "substantial limitation." The impact of this amendment is that it is now easier to establish a disability, and all employees have to do is prove "how any injury or illness affects their ability to perform the job." This is opposed to the earlier test requiring that employees show how their illness and injury was so severe that it even prohibited them from performing major life functions such as walking and brushing their teeth. This means that had Williams sued Toyota today, she would have won!

2. THE DEFINITION OF "MAJOR LIFE FUNCTIONS" HAS BEEN EXPANDED UNDER THE NEW ADA AMENDMENTS

The 2008 amendments have specifically expanded the term "substantial limitation of a major life function" to include the following two nonexhaustive lists:

1.   walking (already recognized by the EEOC) as well as activities such as bending, reading, and communicating (previously not recognized by the EEOC); and

2.   major bodily functions, such as functions of the immune, respiratory, digestive, bowel, bladder, neurological, and circulatory systems.

This expanded list means it is now far easier for an injury or illness to meet the criteria of a "qualifying disability" under the ADA.

CASE 4

Mental and emotional illnesses qualify for Americans with Disabilities Act (ADA) protection.

Case Featured

Thomas M. Mattice v. Memorial Hospital of South Bend
The United States Court of Appeals
(for the Seventh Circuit)
Case No 001364 (2001)

INTRODUCTION

Dr. Thomas Mattice worked as an anesthesiologist with Memorial Hospital when he went on leave for depression and panic disorder. He was then given the OK to return to work without restrictions. Upon returning, Dr. Mattice found that he was subject to more rigorous scrutiny and observation.

Things took a turn for the worse when a patient died in an operating room where Dr. Mattice was the attending anesthesiologist. The hospital swiftly suspended him, and although a peer review panel later recommended that he be allowed to return to work, Memorial refused to budge and later terminated his services.

Dr. Mattice then sued Memorial, but the district court dismissed his complaint on the grounds that it lacked sufficient merits to fall as a disability claim within the ADA. He then appealed this decision before the court of appeals.

WHAT THE COURT HELD

The U.S. Court of Appeals for the Seventh Circuit sided in favor of Dr. Mattice, holding that his disability was protected under the ADA. In its decision that Dr. Mattice qualified for ADA protection, the court stated the following:

"Dr. Mattice also alleged that he had a record of impairment in the major life activities of sleeping, eating, thinking and caring for himself. Because the ADA defines an individual as someone who has a physical or mental impairment that substantially limits one or major life activities, or has a record of such a limitation, Dr. Mattice's allegation of a recode of such an impairment also states a claim under the ADA."

HOW YOU CAN BENEFIT FROM THIS CASE

1. MENTAL ILLNESSES ARE COVERED UNDER THE SCOPE OF THE ADA

To qualify for ADA protection for any mental impairments, an employee will need to show or demonstrate how the mental problem substantially impaired his or her cognitive functions, i.e., his or her ability to think clearly. In proving this, a person will also need to show proof that as a result of this illness, he or she was not able to perform work functions.

2. MAKE THE 2008 ADA AMENDMENTS WORK FOR YOU

Prior to the 2008 amendments, the test for determining whether a person's impairment qualifies for ADA protection was determining if the impairment substantially affected the person's ability to perform "major life functions associated with taking care of oneself"—such as walking, eating, or sleeping. This obviously made it more difficult for a person with depression, for instance, to qualify for ADA protection, as he or she would be regarded as being able to walk, talk, eat, and sleep.

The new law changes this, and all it requires is that a person show how the mental illness (be it bipolar disorder or depression) affected or is affecting his ability to function at work.

CASE 5

The use of sexually charged language at work doesn't necessarily mean sexual harassment

Case Featured

Amaani Lyle v. Warner Brothers Television Productions
**(California Supreme Court)
Case No S125171 (2005)**

INTRODUCTION

Amaani Lyle, a female African American, was elated to find that she had been hired by Warner Brothers as a comedy writers' assistant for the production of the popular television show *Friends*. Four months into the job, she found herself summarily fired on the grounds that her transcription and typing skills were not up to par.

She then filed an action against Warner Brothers and the show's three male comedy writers (Chase, Mallins, and Reich), alleging that their use of sexually coarse and offensive language and conduct, which included recounting their own sexual experiences, constituted sexual harassment within the FEHA or Fair Employment and Housing Act. The following quote from the court provides some insight into the working environment at the *Friends* set.

"In their depositions, Chase, Malins, and Reich gave testimony that corroborated portions of plaintiff's allegations. Chase acknowledges he had discussed, while in the writers' room, his personal sexual experiences. Chase also confirmed that he and other writers discussed anal sex, and that he had gestured on occasion as if he were masturbating, but could not recall having done so when plaintiff was present. Malins and Reich admitted 'blow-job stories' were told in the writers' room. Reich said he also pantomimed masturbation in the writers' room, sometimes as a way of indicating something was a waste of time. In the writers' room and sometimes elsewhere, Reich and other writers discussed oral sex and anal sex, and writers discussed their personal sexual conduct. Reich and others also acknowledged

he and others altered inspirational sayings on a calendar, changing for ex-
ample, the word 'persistence' to 'pert tits' and 'happiness' to 'penis.'"

After losing her case at the state district court, Lyle appealed this decision before the court of appeals, which affirmed the part of the district court's judgment but also concluded that there existed triable issues of fact. Both parties petitioned for a review of this decision before the state supreme court.

WHAT THE COURT HELD

The California Supreme Court found in favor of the defendant (Warner Brothers), ruling that Lyle had failed to prove that she was subject to a hostile work environment or that she had been subject to disparate treatment. In its decision that no disparate treatment had occurred, the court stated:

"Although plaintiff (Lyle) contended in her deposition that much of the three writers' vulgar discussions and conduct wasted her time, there was no indication the conduct affected the work hours or duties of plaintiff and her male counterparts in a disparate manner. Accordingly, while the conduct certainly was tinged with 'sexual content' and 'sexual connotations,' a reasonable trier of fact could not find, based on the facts presented here, that 'members of one sex were exposed to disadvantageous terms or conditions of employment to which members of the opposite sex were not exposed' or that if the plaintiff 'has been a man she would not have been treated in the same manner."

The court also addressed the issue of whether the use of sexually vulgar and coarse language should be outlawed at the workplace. It accordingly stated:

"We do not suggest the use of sexually coarse and vulgar language in the workplace can never constitute harassment because of sex; indeed, language similar to that at issue here might well establish actionable harassment depending on the circumstances. Nor do we imply that employees gen-

erally should be free, without employer restriction, to engage in sexually coarse and vulgar language or conduct at the workplace. We simply recognize that, like Title VII, the FEHA is not a 'civility' code and is not designed to rid the workplace of vulgarity. While the FEHA prohibits harassing conduct that creates a work environment that is hostile or abusive on the basis of sex, it does not outlaw sexually coarse and vulgar language or conduct that merely offends."

HOW YOU CAN BENEFIT FROM THIS CASE

There are two distinct categories of sexual harassment. The first category applies in situations where the nature or circumstances surrounding the harassment is more direct or clear cut—for instance, when your supervisor touches you inappropriately or makes lewd sexual comments directed at you.

The second category, on the other hand, is harder to prove and applies in relatively more indirect circumstances (such as the facts surrounding this case), where the use of sexually coarse language was not directed at offending one particular employee. It is important to know the difference between these two.

If your sexual harassment allegation falls under the second category, there are three key prerequisites you will need to meet. The first is "disparate treatment," where you will need to show proof of how your employer's use of sexually charged language and conduct created a disproportionately negative impact on a particular sex within the organization, be it male or female. This means that not only must you be able to prove that the conduct/language used resulted in the creation of an abusive working environment, but that it disproportionately affected the female or male populace within the company negatively.

The second prerequisite refers to assessing whether the sexually charged language meets the "objective or reasonable person" test. Here, you'll need to show proof that any other rational, thinking person placed in a similar position would have also found the conduct or language used similarly offensive or hostile.

In the third prerequisite, the use of the sexual language or conduct is balanced against a person's fundamental right to free speech under the first amendment. Here, this fundamental right to free speech means that your employer (or its employees) is entitled to use sexually charged language if it can show that it is related to the necessary "creative" pursuits of its work and was not intended to victimize any particular person or sex—as the court found in this case.

Think of how this third requirement applies with the following "contrast" analogy:

Imagine you're working at a shipyard, employed as its only female welder in an otherwise all-male crew, as opposed to working in a museum as a curator where the current display is based on the theme "society's changing views on feminine beauty over the years." If you're subjected to sexually vulgar or offensive comments at the shipyard, you've probably got a solid case—provided, of course, you can prove the hostility and disparate treatment. If you're a female employee at the art museum, on the other hand, you probably could not claim that the comments made by your colleagues on the female physique (when commenting on the naked sculptures displayed) constitute sexual harassment. The key difference here lies in the "context" underlying each situation.

As this second category of sexual harassment can at times be difficult to prove, you may find the relevant quotes by the Supreme Court (from this case) on these three requirements discussed above useful:

On Disparate Treatment

"The record here reflects a workplace where comedy writers were paid to create scripts highlighting adult themed sexual humor and jokes, and where members of both sexes contributed and were exposed to the creative process spawning such humor and jokes. In this context, the defendant writers' non-directed sexual antics and sexual talk did not contribute to an environment in which women and men were treated disparately. Moreover, there was nothing to suggest the defendants engaged

in this particular behavior to make plaintiff uncomfortable or self-conscious, or to intimidate, ridicule, or insult her."

On Objectively Hostile Work Environments

"As the United States Supreme Court has recognized, the prohibition of harassment on the basis of sex requires neither asexuality nor androgyny in the workplace; it forbids only behavior so objectively offensive as to alter the 'conditions of the victim's employment' and create a hostile or abusive working environment. Whether an environment is hostile or abusive can be determined only by looking at all the circumstances including the frequency of the discriminatory conduct; its severity; whether it is physically threatening or humiliating, or a mere offensive utterance; and whether it unreasonably interferes with an employee's work performance.

"Therefore to establish liability in a FEHA hostile work environment sexual harassment case, a plaintiff employee must show she was subjected to sexual advances, conduct, or comments that were severe enough or sufficiently pervasive to alter the conditions of her employment and create a hostile or abusive work environment."

On the First Amendment

"Where, as here, an employer's product is protected by the First Amendment—whether it be a television program, a newspaper, a book, or any other similar work—the challenged speech should not be actionable if the Court finds that the speech arose in the context of the creative and/or editorial process, and it was not directed at or about the plaintiff."

CASE 6

You may still be able to sue for age discrimination despite signing a waiver.

Case Featured

Oubre v. Entergy Operations Inc.
(United States Supreme Court)
Case No 96-1291 (1998)

INTRODUCTION

Oubre worked as a scheduler at a power plant run by Entergy Operations. After receiving a poor performance review, she was told that she could either improve her performance or accept a voluntary severance package. She was given fourteen days to decide whether to accept the severance package. On the fourteenth day, Oubre accepted the severance package, signed a waiver where she agreed to "waive, settle, release, and discharge any and all claims, demands, actions, or causes of action that she may have against Entergy." In return, she received six severance payments over a four-month period.

However, this waiver, drafted by Entergy, violated at least three requirements of the Older Workers Benefits Protection Act (OWBPA), which included:

1. giving Oubre at least twenty-one days to consider the release;
2. providing Oubre with the option of retracting her release within seven days after signing said release; and
3. not making a specific reference to the waiver of her ADEA claims.

After receiving her final settlement, Oubre sued Entergy. Both the state district and appeals court dismissed her case, finding that Oubre had ratified the "defective release" by failing to return her severance pay. She appealed this decision before the state supreme court.

WHAT THE COURT HELD

The United States Supreme Court held in favor of Oubre, reversing the district and court of appeals decision. In its decision, the court clarified that the OWBPA's standards for obtaining a waiver are absolute and any nonconformance to those standards means that the waiver is automatically deemed ineffective. The court stated as follows in articulating its position:

"The statutory command is clear. An employee may not waive an ADEA claim unless the waiver or release satisfies the OWBPA's requirements. The OWBPA implements Congress policy via a strict, unqualified statutory stricture on waivers, and we are bound to take Congress at its word. Congress imposed specific duties on employers who seek releases of certain claims created by statute. Congress delineated these duties with precision and without qualification: An employee 'may not waive' an ADEA claim unless the employer complies with the statute."

In further supporting its decision, the court also opined that an employee that has lost a job may have already spent the severance money (in exchange for the waiver) and may therefore lack the means to return it. It accordingly quoted the following:

"Realities might tempt employers to risk noncompliance with the OWBPA's waiver provisions, knowing it will be difficult to repay the monies and relying on ratification. We ought not to open the door to an evasion of the statute by this device."

HOW YOU CAN BENEFIT FROM THIS CASE

I.   THE LAW IS ON YOUR SIDE WITH ADEA WAIVERS

Any employer wanting to obtain a valid release under the ADEA (Age Discrimination of Employment Act) needs to comply with all the requirements spelt forth by the OWBPA. If your employer fails to fulfill any of these requirements, the law is on your side, and you can still sue despite not returning the severance pay you earlier received.

2. KNOW THE ADEA WAIVER REQUIREMENTS

The Older Workers Benefits Protection Act has a clause which specifies that in order for an ADEA waiver to be valid, it must be made knowingly and willingly. This waiver or "golden handshake." as it is commonly called, must meet the following seven requirements, without which it is deemed not applicable:

1. The agreement must be in writing and easy to understand.
2. It specifically refers to what your ADEA rights and claims are.
3. It must contain something of value in exchange that is in addition to what you are already entitled to under the law or company policy.
4. It cannot waive any rights or entitlements that may arise after the date of the waiver.
5. It must state your rights to consult an attorney before signing the waiver.
6. It must state that you are given at least twenty-one days to sign the waiver.
7. It must state that you are permitted to revoke the agreement for up to seven days after signing it.

CASE 7

Your employer cannot discriminate on the basis of gender when recruiting, promoting, or terminating.

Case Featured

Burlington Northern & Santa Fe Railway Co. v. White
(The United States Supreme Court)
Case No 05-259 (2006)

INTRODUCTION

When Sheila White, the only female employee working in the Maintenance of Way department at Burlington, complained to company officials that her supervisor, Bill Joiner, had made inappropriate and insulting remarks to her in front of her male colleagues, the company responded by suspending him for ten days. White was informed of Joiner's discipline but also told that they were removing her from forklift duty and that she was reassigned to performing standard laborer tasks. Burlington further informed her that the reassignment reflected her co-workers' views that forklift duties (which were a less arduous and cleaner task) should be given to a more "senior man."

White filed an EEOC complaint while continuing to work for Burlington. When she later found that she was placed under surveillance and monitored on a daily basis, she filed a second retaliatory suit with the EEOC. A few days later, White was suspended without pay after disagreeing with another supervisor, Percy Sharkey, over which truck should transport her from one location to another. White launched a grievance over this suspension, which led to the company finding that she had not been insubordinate and reinstating her to her position with back pay for the thirty-seven days she was suspended.

Following this, White filed an additional retaliation charge with the EEOC for this suspension before suing Burlington at federal district court. Both the federal district and full court of appeals found in her favor and awarded her $43,500 in compensatory damages, including $3,250 in medical expenses. Burlington appealed these decisions to the federal Supreme Court.

WHAT THE COURT HELD

The United States Supreme Court found in White's favor. In its decision, the court found that Burlington's decision to reassign her from performing forklift work to doing track labor duties was materially adverse to White *despite there being no reduction in her pay*. It accordingly stated the following:

> **"To be sure, reassignment of job duties is not automatically actionable. Whether a particular reassignment is materially adverse depends upon the circumstances of the particular case, and 'should be judged from the perspective of a reasonable person in the plaintiff's position, considering 'all the circumstances.' But here, the jury had before it considerable evidence that track labor duties were 'by all accounts more arduous and dirtier'; that the forklift operator position required more qualification, which is an indication of prestige; and that the forklift operator position was objectively considered a better job and the male employee resented White for occupying it. Based on this record, a jury could reasonable conclude that the reassignment of responsibilities would have been materially adverse to a reasonable employee."**

The court also dismissed Burlington's assertion that White had no legal rights given that the company had already paid her back for the earlier thirty-seven days' suspension (without pay). The court accordingly quoted the following in addressing this issue:

> **"White did receive back pay. But White and her family had to live for 37 days without income. They did not know during that time whether or when White could return to work. Many reasonable employees would find a month without a paycheck to be serious hardship. And White de-**

scribed to the jury the physical and emotional hardship that 37 days of having 'no income, no money' in fact caused. ('That was the worst Christmas I had out of my life. No income, no money, and they made all of us feel bad...I got very depressed') Indeed, she obtained medical treatment for her emotional distress. A reasonable employee facing the choice between retaining her job (and paycheck) and filing a discrimination lawsuit complaint might well choose the former. That is to say, an indefinite suspension without pay could well act as a deterrent, even if the suspended employee eventually received back pay. It needs no argument to show that fear of economic retaliation might often operate to induce aggrieved employees quietly to accept substandard conditions. Thus, the jury's conclusion that the 37 day suspension was materially adverse was a reasonable one."

HOW YOU CAN BENEFIT FROM THIS CASE

I. MONEY ISNT THE ONLY CRITERIA FOR PROVING DISCRIMINATION

Where your employer reassigns you to a position you deem lower in rank, you still have legal rights despite your salary remaining intact. What you will need to prove is that the new position amounts to a demotion, and, if you are able to establish this, the court will rule in your favor—as it did with Sheila White.

Section 703(a) of the Civil Rights Act is relevant to quote here, as it aptly summarizes what your employer is prohibited from doing:

"It shall be an unlawful employment practice for an employer (1) to fail or refuse to hire or discharge any individual, or otherwise to discriminate against any individual with respect to his compensation, terms, conditions, or privileges of employment, because of such individual's race, color, religion, sex or national origin; or (2) to limit, segregate, or classify his employees or applicants for employment in any way which would deprive or tend to deprive any individual of employment opportunities

or otherwise adversely affect his status as an employee, because of such individual's race, color, religion, sex or national origin."

2. YOUR EMPLOYER HAD BETTER NOT RETALIATE

If you find that you've been reassigned due to a complaint you earlier raised, be it a safety violation, Title VII discrimination or for sexual harassment, the law is on your side. More laws are being drafted protecting employees from employer recriminations. Sarbanes-Oxley, for instance, is one such recent law that has been passed to protect whistle-blowers reporting accounting- and securities-related fraud to the authorities.

Despite these laws' existence, it is still best that you document any incident or form of retaliation you are subjected to. In this regard, once you have initiated the process, keep filing any additional retaliation complaints with the authorities in building on your evidence.

3. KNOW THE STANDARD USED BY THE COURTS TO DETERMINE IF RETALIATION HAS TAKEN PLACE

The human capacity for ingenuity is limitless, and when an employer-employee relationship hits testy waters, you'll find that your employer may have a host of means and ways to subtly retaliate against you. As these means and ways can come in so many different forms, the courts don't have a definitive list of what does and doesn't constitute retaliation. It instead will adopt the *"reasonable employee standard" test*, as was the case here, where the court stated the following:

"The real social impact of workplace behavior often depends on a constellation of surrounding circumstances, expectations, and relationships which are not fully captured by a simple recitation of the words used or the physical acts performed. A schedule change in an employee's work schedule may make little difference to many workers, but may matter enormously to a young mother with school age children. A supervisor's refusal to invite an employee to lunch is normally trivial, a nonactionable petty plight. But to retaliate by excluding an employee

from a weekly training lunch that contributes significantly to the employee's professional advancement might well deter a reasonable employee from complaining about discrimination."

Think of this "reasonable employee standard test" as the court asking the following question:

"Would a reasonable or objective, thinking person placed in the same situation also feel similarly retaliated against?"

CASE 8

In cases involving unfair discrimination, an employee may in certain circumstances be entitled to more than $300,000.

Case Featured

Pollard v. E. I. du Pont de Nemours & Co.
(United States Supreme Court)
Case No 00-763 (2001)

INTRODUCTION

When Sharon Pollard sued her employer, E. I. du Pont, for sexual harassment, the district court found in her favor, ruling that she had been subject to a sexually hostile working environment. The court also awarded Pollard $107,364 in back pay and benefits, $252,997 in attorney fees, and $300,000 (the maximum permitted by law) as compensatory damages. Pollard was unsatisfied with this award and felt that the $300,000 cap for compensatory damages should not apply in her situation as she was entitled to "front pay"—a replacement income in lieu of her being reinstated to her job. When the court of appeals declined to intervene, Pollard took this matter before the Supreme Court.

WHAT IS FRONT PAY?

Front pay is the money awarded as compensation by the courts in lieu of reinstating the employee back to his or her former job. It is usually awarded in situations where the court finds that reinstating the employee to the former position is no longer possible due to the tenuous or strained relationship existing between the employer and employee. Front pay can also be awarded in situations where the position formerly held by the employee has now been filled or is no longer available within the organization.

WHAT THE COURT HELD

The United States Supreme Court held in Pollard's favor, finding that front pay was not a component of compensatory damages and was therefore *not part of the statutory cap of $300,000*. In its decision that front pay could not be considered part of compensatory damages, the court stated the following:

> **"Section 1981a(a)(1) provides that, in intentional discrimination cases brought under Title VII, 'the complaining party may recover compensatory and punitive damages as allowed under subsection (b) of (1981a), in addition to any relief authorized by section 706(g) of the Civil Rights Act of 1964. And s. 1981(b)(2) states that compensatory damages awarded under s.(1981a) shall not include back pay, interest on back pay, or any other type of relief authorized under section 706(g) of the Civil Rights Act of 1964. According to these statutory provisions, if front pay was a type of statutory relief authorized under s.706(g), it is excluded from the meaning of compensatory damages under s.1981a."**

HOW YOU CAN BENEFIT FROM THIS CASE

FRONT PAY IS NOT PART OF THE $300,000 CAP

If your employer is found guilty for a Title VII civil rights violation, the statutory limit of $300,000 does not apply for any front pay awarded. This means that if you can prove discrimination and are found entitled to front pay, you could be looking at a payout north of $300,000. Front-pay awards are particularly common in sexual harassment suits, where the courts find placing the employee back in his or her formerly hostile working environment to be impractical.

CASE 9

The Civil Rights Act may still apply to employers who don't meet the minimum fifteen-employee threshold.

Case Featured

Walters v. Metropolitan Educational Enterprises, Inc.
(The United States Supreme Court)
Case Nos. 950259 & 95-779 (1997)

INTRODUCTION

When Darleen Walters filed a gender discrimination complaint against her employer, Metropolitan, it responded by firing her. She proceeded to sue the company. Metropolitan, however, filed a motion to dismiss her suit on the basis that since it did not employ more than fifteen employees, Title VII of the Civil Rights Act didn't apply to it.

Both the district court and court of appeals agreed with Metropolitan, holding that the correct formula to determine whether an employer meets the minimum fifteen-employee threshold test is determined by calculating the days on which employees of the organization actually perform work or were compensated when they were absent. Walters challenged this decision before the Supreme Court.

This case is important as it answers the critically important question of how the courts determine whether an employer has fifteen or more employees working for him for at least twenty calendar weeks in any current or preceding calendar year, as stipulated in the act.

WHAT THE COURT HELD

The Supreme Court found in favor of Walters, holding that the correct test to determine whether an employer has fifteen or more employees working for it over at least twenty weeks is to look at its payroll records, i.e., to determine whether the employee(s) was on the company payroll during the period in question. In determining that the correct fifteen-employee threshold test is the "payroll method," the Court stated the following:

"We think that the payroll method represents the fair reading of the statutory language, which sets as the criterion the number of employees that the employer 'has' for each working day. In common parlance, an employer has an employee if he maintains an employment relationship with that individual."

Metropolitan's argument in this case was that the correct test should be who the employer had actually working for him on that particular day, and not whom he has under his payroll. The court, in dismissing this argument, stated the following:

"Metropolitan contends that if one were asked how many employees he had for a given working day, he would give as the answer the number of employees who are actually performing work on that day. That is possibly so. Language is a subtle enough thing that the phrase' have an employee for a given working day' maybe thought to convey the idea that the employee must actually be working on the day in question. But no-one before us urges that interpretation of the language, which would count even salaried employees only on days that they are actually working. Such a disposition is so improbable and so impossible to administer that (few employers keep daily attendance records of all their salaried employees) Congress should be thought to have prescribed it only if the language could bear no other meaning."

HOW YOU CAN BENEFIT FROM THIS CASE

In determining whether your employer is covered under Title VII, use the Payroll Method.

The payroll method assesses how many employees the employer has under its payroll during the day or period in question, and the courts have ruled that this method is by far the most practical way to determine whether your employer is covered under Title VII. This case has thrown out arguments by employers that may have in the past hidden from discrimination claims by claiming that the correct test for determining coverage is whether they had fifteen employees physically working for them during the day or period in question.

CASE 10

Having a sexual relationship with one's supervisor doesn't preclude an employee from later claiming sexual harassment against the organization.

Case Featured

Meritor Savings Bank v. Vinson
The United States Supreme Court
Case No 84-179 (1986)

INTRODUCTION

When Michelle Vinson applied for a position at Meritor Savings Bank, she met with Sydney Taylor, its vice president. She was subsequently hired and within a period of four years progressed from the position of teller-trainee to assistant branch manager—with Taylor as her supervisor. Around four years into her employment, Vinson notified Taylor that she was taking sick leave for an indefinite period, which led to the bank terminating her services for taking excessive leave.

Vinson then brought an action against Taylor and the bank where she alleged that during her four years there, she was subject to constant sexual harassment by Taylor in violation of Title VII. During the trial, allegations emerged that she and Taylor had been having sexual relations, with Vinson estimating that over several years she had intercourse with him some forty to fifty times. Taylor denied all the respondent's allegations of sexual activity. The bank also denied any liability, stating that Vinson had never informed them of any sexual harassment by Taylor.

When the federal district court held in favor of the bank, Vinson challenged its decision before the federal court of appeals which held that the harassment by her supervisor (Taylor) created a hostile working environment which was covered under Title VII. The Court of Appeals also stated that *"if Taylor had made Vinson's toleration of sexual harassment a condition, the fact of whether she had submitted to it does not alter the fact that it is still sexual harassment."* The court also held that Meritor would also be liable, irrespective of whether it knew about the harassment.

Meritor appealed this decision before the federal Supreme Court.

WHAT THE COURT HELD

The United States Supreme Court found in Vinson's favor that she had been sexually harassed and was entitled to Title VII protection. In its decision, the court stated that the fact that Taylor and Vinson engaged in a sexual relationship did not mean that no sexual harassment had taken place. It accordingly stated the following:

"The correct enquiry is whether respondent by her conduct indicated that the alleged sexual advances were unwelcome, not whether her actual participation in intercourse was voluntary. The EEOC guidelines emphasize that the try of fact must determine the existence of sexual harassment in light of 'record as a whole' and the totality of circumstances, such as the nature of the sexual advances and the contacts in which the alleged incidents occurred."

The court also found that the existence of the company's grievance procedure and policy against discrimination were not enough to insulate Meritor from liability. The court accordingly stated the following in finding that the bank was liable for Taylor's sexual harassment:

"The bank's general non-discrimination policy did not address sexual harassment in particular and thus did not alert employees to their employer's interest in correcting that form of discrimination. Moreover, the bank's grievance procedure apparently required an employee to complain first to her supervisor, in this case Taylor. Since Taylor was the alleged perpetrator it is not altogether surprising that respondent failed to invoke the procedure and report her grievance to him. Petitioner's (the bank's) contention that respondent's failure should insulate it from liability might be substantially stronger if its procedures were better calculated to encourage victims of harassment to come forward."

HOW YOU CAN BENEFIT FROM THIS CASE

1. SUBMISSION DOES NOT NECESSARILY MEAN IT'S VOLUNTARY

Most sexual harassment cases deal with harassment before an actual act of intercourse has taken place. This case decision demonstrates that an employee's submission to a supervisor's demands for sex doesn't mean this person has lost any Title VII protection for sexual harassment either. In Vinson's situation, the Court stated that the test for determining whether Title VII applies isn't whether the employee voluntarily submitted to it, but whether there was clear indication that the "*sexual advances were unwelcome and created a hostile working environment.*"

2. HAVING A GRIEVANCE POLICY DOESN'T ALWAYS ABSOLVE THE EMPLOYER

The existence of a grievance policy doesn't necessarily absolve an employer for any sexual harassment acts committed by its supervisors. While it's certainly a prerequisite for mitigation, your employer must also be able to show:

1. it had a specific process for managing sexual harassment that was communicated to employees; and
2. that immediate action was taken to correct or avoid any sexual harassment claims raised.

In short, if you feel your employer's policy isn't clear enough or hasn't been clearly communicated to its employees or that your employer failed to take immediate corrective/remedial action upon receiving your complaint, you've still got Title VII protection.

CASE 11

You may still be able to sue your ex-employer under the Civil Rights Act if it gives you a poor job reference.

Case Featured

Robinson v. Shell Oil Company
The United States Supreme Court
Case No 95-1376 (1997)

INTRODUCTION

When Charles T. Robinson found he had been fired by the Shell Oil Company, he lodged an EEOC complaint alleging that the true reason behind his termination was due to his race. Robinson then started looking for a job, and when his prospective employers contacted Shell for a reference, they responded by providing Robinson with a poor reference. Robinson then lodged a Title VII civil rights action against Shell, alleging that they gave him a negative reference in retaliation for his filing his EEOC complaint.

The federal district court, while finding evidence of "retaliatory" conduct by Shell, held that Robinson had no legal recourse as Title VII protection did not extend to *"former"* employees. In basing its decision, the court found that the fact that Robinson had already been fired when he lodged a complaint meant that he was not an employee within the purview of Title VII protection. This finding was also echoed by the court of appeals, leading Robinson to challenge this decision before the Supreme Court.

WHAT THE COURT HELD

The U.S. Supreme Court held in favor of Robinson, finding that Section 704 (a) of Title VII of the Civil Rights Act extends to former employees. The Court quoted these two statements in its findings that

Robinson was still protected under the Civil Rights Act despite being a former employee:

Quote 1

"Finding that the term 'employees' in Section 704 (a) is ambiguous, we are left to resolve that ambiguity. The broader context provided by other sections of the statute provides considerable assistance in this regard. As noted above, several sections of the statute plainly contemplate that former employees will make use of the remedial mechanisms of Title VII. Indeed Section 703(a) expressly includes discriminatory 'discharge' as one of the unlawful employment practices against which Title VII is directed. Insofar as Section 704 (a) expressly protects employees from retaliation for filing a 'charge' under Title VII, and a charge under Section 703(a) alleging unlawful discharge would necessarily be brought by a former employee, it is far more consistent to include former employees within the scope of 'employees' protected by Section 704 (a)."

Quote 2

"In further support of this view, petitioner argues that the word 'employees' includes former employees because to hold otherwise would effectively vitiate much of the protection afforded by Section 704(a). This is also the position taken by EEOC. According to EEOC, exclusion of former employees from the protection of Section 704(a) would undermine the effectiveness of Title VII by allowing the threat of post employment retaliation to deter victims of discrimination from complaining to EEOC, and would provide a perverse incentive for employers to fire employees who might bring Title VII claims."

HOW YOU CAN BENEFIT FROM THIS CASE

YOU ARE PROTECTED UNDER TITLE VII OF THE CIVIL RIGHTS ACT FOR POSTEMPLOYMENT RETALIATION

This decision shows that your employer cannot give you a negative job reference after you have left the organization and filed a Title VII charge. In its rationale that Title VII includes former employees, the Court opined that unless it extended protection to them, employers would be free to use the threat of retaliation to deter employees from lodging Title VII complaints. Here is what it stated with regard to this issue of postemployment retaliation:

"Allowing the threat of post employment retaliation to deter victims of discrimination from complaining to the EEOC would provide a perverse incentive for employers to fire employees who might bring Title VII claims."

CASE 12

You are protected by Title VII even if you are white.

Case Featured

Ricci et al. v. DeSteffano et al.
The United States Supreme Court
Case No 07-1428 (2009)

INTRODUCTION

In 2003, the City of New Haven, Connecticut, used objective ex-aminations to identify firefighters best qualified for promotion. One hundred eighteen New Haven firefighters took these examinations, which would qualify them for promotion to the rank of lieutenant and captain. A total of seventy-seven candidates sat for the lieutenant examination, which thirty-four of them passed—of which twenty-five were whites. Forty-one candidates also passed the captain examina-tion, of which twenty-five were whites.

As the test results showed that the white candidates had vast-ly out-performed minority candidates, the city chose to ignore the test results, consequently denying promotion to the candidates who had done well. This led certain whites and one Hispanic firefighter who likely would have been promoted due to their good test results to sue the city and some of its officials. The basis of their suit was that the city had, by discarding the test results, discriminated against them on the basis of their race, in violation of both Title VII of the Civil Rights Act and the Equal Protection Clause of the Fourteenth Amendment.

The City defended its actions by arguing that it would have prob-ably faced a Title VII suit by the minority firefighters (on grounds of disparate impact) had it certified the test results. Both the dis-trict court and court of appeals sided with the City, leading to the plaintiffs appealing this decision before the United States Supreme Court.

WHAT THE COURT HELD

The United States Supreme Court found in favor of the plaintiffs (firefighters), holding that the city's justification for throwing out the examination results was wrong. In this decision, the Court stated the following:

> *"The City's race-based rejection of the test results cannot satisfy the strong-basis-in-evidence standard. The racial adverse impact in this litigation was significant, and petitioners do not dispute that the City was faced with a prima facie case of disparate-impact liability. The problem for respondents is that such a prima facie case – essentially, a threshold showing of a significant statistical disparity and nothing more - is far from a strong basis in evidence that the City would have been liable under Title VII had it certified the test results. That is because the City could be liable for disparate-impact discrimination only if <u>the exams at issue were not job related and consistent with business necessity,</u> or if there existed an equally valid, less discriminatory alternative that served the City's needs but that the City refused to adopt Section 2000e-2(k)(1)(A), (C). Based on the record the parties developed through discovery, there is no substantial evidence that the test was deficient in either respect."*

In refuting the City's assertion that it had no other choice but to disregard the test results, the court pointed out that the City had not shown that there were other less discriminatory, equally valid testing alternatives available that it could have adopted. The Court accordingly stated the following:

> *"Respondents also lack a strong basis in evidence showing an equally valid, less discriminatory testing alternative that the City, by certifying the test results, would necessarily have refused to adopt. Respondents' three arguments to the contrary all fail. First, respondents refer to testimony that a different composite-score calculation would have allowed the City to consider black candidates for then-open positions, but they have produced no evidence to show that the candidate weighting actually used was indeed arbitrary, or that the different weighting would be an equally valid way to determine whether candidates are qualified for promotions.*

"Second, respondents argue that the City could have adopted a different interpretation of its charter provision limiting promotions to the highest scoring applicants, and that the interpretation would have produced less discriminatory results; but respondent's approach would have violated Title VII's prohibition of race-based adjustment of test results, Section 2000e-3(l). Third, testimony asserting that the use of an assessment center to evaluate candidates' behavior in typical job tasks would have had less adverse impact than written exams does not aid respondents, as it is contradicted by other statements in the record indicating that the City could not have used assessment centers for the exams at issue. Especially when it is noted that the strong-basis-in-evidence standard applies to this case, respondents cannot create a genuine issue of fact based on a few stray (and contradictory) statements in the record."

HOW YOU CAN BENEFIT FROM THIS CASE

I. FEAR OF LITIGATION ALONE CANNOT JUSTIFY RACIAL DISCRIMINATION, BE IT DIRECT OR REVERSE

Your employer can't apply the reason that it is fearful of being sued by other minority employees as a basis for ignoring any test results that would put a nonminority in an advantageous position for hiring or promotion. When your employer wants to disregard the test or assessment scores, it must first satisfy the strong basis in evidence standard (see below).

2. KNOW WHAT THE STRONG BASIS IN EVIDENCE STANDARD MEANS

An employee can only sue his or her employer under "disparate impact" discrimination (in relation to test/examinations administered) if he or she is able to prove that:

I.   the tests were not job related or consistent with business necessity;

2.   there existed an equally valid, less discriminatory alternative that served the employer's needs, but the employer refused to adopt it.

These two requirements are what are called "the strong basis in evidence standard" (in context of this case). Since the City was unable to prove that there were other less discriminatory tests available or that the exam questions were not job related, the court found that the minority employees, in any case, would not have succeeded in any claim for disparate impact—meaning that the city's decision to disregard the examination results was wrong.

3. THE DIFFERENCE BETWEEN "DISPARATE IMPACT" AND "DISPARATE TREATMENT"

Disparate impact occurs when an apparently neutral policy has a disproportionately negative impact on one or more employees under a protected class. For example, the City's examination test *could* potentially have been said to have had a disparate impact on its minority firefighters.

Disparate treatment, on the other hand, occurs where an employer intentionally treats an employee differently because of his or her race, color, religion, age, or any other category protected by law. In our featured case, the white and Hispanic employees who had scored high on the firefighters' examinations claimed disparate treatment, as they felt the City had intentionally treated them differently by ignoring their test scores—a point that the U.S. Supreme Court concurred with.

CASE 13

You don't need to be the person initiating a sexual harass-ment complaint to be protected by the law.

Case Featured

Crawford v. Metropolitan Government of Nashville and Davidson County, Tennessee
United States Court of Appeal for the Sixth Circuit
Case No 06-1595 (2008)

INTRODUCTION

When rumors of sexual harassment by its employee relations direc-tor, named Hughes, surfaced, the local government (Metro) for the state of Tennessee convened its internal investigation. During these investigations, a subordinate of Hughes, named Crawford, revealed that he had sexually harassed her.

However, instead of firing Hughes, Metro fired Crawford—osten-sibly on grounds of embezzlement. Crawford then sued Metro on the basis that it had retaliated against her for reporting Hughes's behavior. Metro contended that Crawford was not entitled to any Title VII re-course as she had not initiated any complaint of sexual harassment prior to the investigation.

The district and appeals courts, however, found in favor of Metro, holding that Title VII protection did not apply to her as she had not ac-tively or consistently "opposed" the sexual harassment allegedly com-mitted by her supervisor, Hughes. Dissatisfied, Crawford appealed this decision before the Supreme Court.

WHAT THE COURT HELD

The U.S. Supreme Court found in favor of Crawford, holding that the law did not require her to be the person initiating the complaint to prove she opposed the alleged sexual harassment. In its decision, the Court stated:

"When an employee communicates to her employer a belief that the employer has engaged in...a form of employment discrimination, that communication 'virtually always' constitutes the employee's opposition to the activity."

The Court also deliberated on what an employee is required to do in proving that he or she "opposed" any form of sexual harassment he or she was subject to. stating:

" 'Oppose' goes beyond 'active, consistent' behavior in ordinary discourse, where we would naturally use the word to speak of someone who has taken no action at all to advance a position beyond disclosing it. Countless people were known to 'oppose' slavery before Emancipation, or are said to 'oppose' capital punishment today, without writing public letters, taking to the streets, or resisting the Government. And we would call it 'opposition' if an employee took a stand against an employers discriminatory practices not by 'instigating' action, but by standing pat, say, by refusing to follow a superior's order to fire a junior worker for discriminatory reasons. Cf. McDonnel, supra, at 262 (finding employee covered by Title VII of the Civil Rights Act of 1964 where his employer retaliated against him for failing to prevent his subordinate from filing an EEOC charge).

"There is then, no reason to doubt that a person can 'oppose' by responding to someone else's question just as surely as by provoking the discussion, and nothing in the statute requires a freakish rule protecting an employee who reports discrimination on her own initiative but not one who reports the same discrimination in the same words when her boss asks a question."

HOW YOU CAN BENFIT FROM THIS CASE

To meet the law's requirement for "opposition," you needn't be the person initiating the complaint. As the court stated in this case, an employee can oppose by responding to another person's question as well as by provoking the discussion.

CASE 14

You may still be entitled to overtime despite occupying a job position labeled as "administrative" or "managerial."

Case Featured

Pellegrino v. Robert Half International, Inc.
(California Court of Appeals—Fourth Circuit)
Case No G040762 (2010)

INTRODUCTION

Maria Pellegrino and five of her colleagues worked for Robert Half International (RHI), a recruitment company that focused on placing temporary employees in the legal, accounting, finance, creative, and office team divisions of its client organizations. When RHI didn't pay them their overtime, commissions, or meal period allowance, or provide them with itemized wage statements, the six of them alleged that their employer had violated wage and hour laws under the Fair Labor Standards Act and initiated legal action.

In contending that their six employees had no basis to support their allegations, RHI asserted that:

1)   as all six employees had signed a "limitation on claims" agreement upon joining RHI, they were barred from pursuing any compensation in excess of six months; and
2)   since the plaintiffs were employed in administrative, executive, professional, and sales capacities, they were exempt from wage and hour laws under the FLSA.

The superior court of Orange County found in favor of the six employees, ruling that the "limitation on claims" clause in their employment contract was unfair and unenforceable. In addition, the court also concluded that since they did not work within an administrative capacity, they were covered under wage and hour laws and entitled to their overtime, commission, and meal period allowance. RHI appealed this decision.

WHAT THE COURT HELD

The California Court of Appeals affirmed the superior court's decision. In agreeing that the "limitation clause" of six months was not enforceable, it quoted the following:

"Here, RHI classified each plaintiff as an exempt employee and, because of that classification, did not pay overtime wages or comply with other wage and hour statutes. Enforcement of a provision, such as the limitation on claims provision in this case, would result in barring legitimate, unwaivable statutory wage and hour claims asserted by misclassified employees who are unable to recover their employer's classification error and assert appropriate claims within six months of the date their employment ended. We conclude this provision contravenes the vindication of such statutory rights within the meaning of and in violation of section 219 and violates the fundamental public policies, underlying each right."

The court then dealt with the issue of whether the plaintiffs were employed under the category of "administrative employees"—which would mean they were not entitled to the overtime, commissions, and meal periods they were claiming (in addition to their right to an itemized wage statement). In finding that they did not fall within the "administrative" category defined under the FLSA, the court stated the following:

"The phrase 'directly related to management policies or general business operations of his employer or his employer's customers' describes those types of activities relating to the administrative operations of a business as distinguished from 'production' or, in the retail or service establishment, 'sales' work. In addition to describing the type of activities, the phrase limits the exemption to persons who perform work of substantial importance to the management or operation of the business of his employer or his employer's customers.

"Here, substantial evidence showed plaintiffs' duties as account executives for RHI were not directly related to management policies because they instead constituted sales work. The evidence presented at trial included the following:1) at RHI, a direct sale occurred when a candidate was placed with a client; 2) account executives were trained in sales and evaluated on how well they met or exceeded minimum sales production numbers; 3) account executives were primarily responsible for selling the services of RHI's temporary employees to clients; 4) when the account executives were not soliciting potential clients for sales or placing orders for clients, they were recruiting more candidates for RHI's inventory, an activity that consumed about 30 percent of their time; 5) account executives had no role in supervising the temporary employees after they were placed and had no responsibility for the administrative support staff in the account executives offices; 6) account executives did form policy but followed the 'recipe', including the three week rotation system in performing their duties as required by headquarters; and 7) corporate headquarters included a human resources department, marketing department, and legal department designed to support the account executives function—to focus on making sales."

HOW YOU CAN BENEFIT FROM THIS CASE

1. LIMITATION CLAUSES CANNOT TRUMP THE LAW

Your employer cannot enforce any "limitation clause" you signed in your employment agreement limiting your rights to pursue compensation against it. Even if you sign one, the law still protects you, as this case has shown.

2. The TEST FOR DETERMINING IF YOU PERFORM "ADMINISTRATIVE" WORK

Title 8 of the California Code of Regulations provides a five-part test to determine whether the administrative exemption applies. Just because you're not based in California doesn't mean this regulation doesn't apply, as most courts in other states will adopt a similar criteria. The test to determine if an employee falls under the "administrative" category is that he or she:

1. must perform office or nonmanual work directly related to management policies or general business operations of the employer or its clients;
2. customarily and regularly exercise discretion and independent judgment;
3. perform only general supervision work where the work involved is along specialized or technical lines requiring special training;
4. be engaged in activities in meeting the test of exemption (i.e., nonmanual) at least 50 percent of the time; and
5. earn twice the state's minimum wage.

3.   IT IS THE JOB FUNCTION, NOT THE JOB POSITION

Some firms may be tempted to try to escape the need to comply with wage and hour laws by labeling their employees under a management or administrative category despite the reality of the job duties and functions being far different. If you find yourself in a situation where you're labeled as managerial or administrative level despite your actual work duties containing no such (administrative or managerial) element, you do have legal rights.

RHI discovered this when the court ruled that since the six employees' work functions did not involve work directly related to policy making or decisions pertaining to general business operations, they didn't fall under the "exempt" employee category—meaning that they are protected by wage and hour laws and entitled to the overtime, commissions, and meal period allowances they were seeking.

CASE 15

Sarbanes-Oxley protects you even where you only suspect fraud.

Case Featured

Shawn and Lena Van Asdale v. International Game Technology
(United States Court of Appeals – for the Ninth Circuit)
Case No 07-16597 (2009)

INTRODUCTION

The husband and wife team of Shawn and Lena Van Asdale were initially hired by International Game Technology (IGT) as their associate general counsel. They progressed steadily within the organization, where they occupied their last-held positions of director of strategic development and director of IP procurement, respectively.

Trouble started when IGT began negotiations with a company called Anchor Gaming on a potential merger. During discussions, it became known that a "wheel patent," which constituted a valuable part of Anchor Gaming's holdings, was embroiled in patent litigation with its competitor, Bally Gaming. Nevertheless, despite this potential lawsuit, the merger was pushed through by IGT's inner circle, and IGT was subsequently awarded the patent in 2003.

Postmerger, Shawn Van Asdale became aware of the existence of an "Australian Flyer" patent that would have had the effect of invalidating the 2003 patent awarded to IGT and deeming Anchor's wheel patent (which formed a substantial portion of the company's valuation) invalid. Shawn then informed IGT's general counsel (Brown) of his view that the litigation against Bally could not go forward and expressed his concern that the Australian Flyer had not been disclosed by Anchor to IGT prior to the merger.

In the meantime, management changes had taken placed postmerger in which a person named Johnson (Anchor's former general counsel) was named to replace Brown as general counsel for IGT. On

November 24, 2003, Shawn and Lena met with Johnson and voiced their concerns. Within a few months of this meeting, both Shawn and Lena found themselves terminated.

The Van Asdales sued IGT using the whistle-blower protection provisions of Sarbanes-Oxley in federal district court. IGT, in turn, launched a motion for summary judgment on the grounds that the Van Asdales were prohibited in law from pursuing any claim, on the grounds of attorney-client privilege. When the district court agreed with IGT, the Van Asdales appealed this decision before the present court of appeals.

WHAT THE COURT HELD

The U.S. Court of Appeals (for the Ninth District) reversed the district court's judgment, finding that the Van Asdales were not prohibited from pursuing their case under Sarbanes-Oxley on the grounds of attorney-client privilege. In its decision, the court quoted the following:

"Section 1514A(b) of Sarbanes-Oxley expressly authorizes any 'person' alleging discrimination based on protected conduct to file a complaint with the Secretary of Labor and, thereafter, to bring suit in an appropriate district court. Nothing in this section indicates that in-house attorneys are not also protected from retaliation under this section, even though Congress plainly considered the role attorneys might play in reporting possible securities fraud. We thus disagree with the district court that dismissal of the Van Asdales' claim on grounds of attorney-client privilege is unwarranted."

The Court also dealt with the issue of whether the Van Asdales were required to "prove their claim of fraud" before they could be covered under Sarbanes-Oxley provisions. It accordingly quoted the following:

"It is not critical to the Van Asdales' claim that they prove that Anchor officials actually engaged in fraud in connection with the merger; rather, the Van Asdales only need show that

they reasonably believed that there might have been fraud and were fired for even suggesting further inquiry. To encourage disclosure, Congress chose statutory language which ensures that 'an employee's reasonable but mistaken belief that an employer engaged in conduct that constitutes a violation of one of the six enumerated categories below is protected."

HOW YOU CAN BENEFIT FROM THIS CASE

1. EMPLOYERS CANNOT ESCAPE SARBANES-OXLEY ON THE GROUNDS OF ATTORNEY-CLIENT PRIVILEGE

The court made very clear that the underlying objective of Sarbanes Oxley is to protect any person who brings up a protected complaint from being discriminated against. The six categories of fraud reporting protected under Sarbanes-Oxley are (a) mail fraud, (b) wire fraud, (c) bank fraud, (d) securities fraud, (e) breach of any Securities and Exchange Commission rule or regulation, and (f) fraud against shareholders under any federal law—and any employee reporting under any of these six categories is automatically protected.

2. YOU DONT HAVE TO ESTABLISH THAT THE FRAUD ACTUALLY OCCURRED IN ORDER TO DERIVE SARBANES-OXLEY PROTECTION

Proving the fraud actually occurred isn't a prerequisite for Sarbanes-Oxley protection. Congress, in encouraging people to come forth and report violations, have clarified (in drafting the law) that all that is required is "any conduct that the employee *reasonably believes* constitutes a violation" of the six categories. In essence, all you need to establish is that you reasonably believed that a violation or fraud was committed!

CASE 16

Your right to freedom of speech is not unfettered.

Case Featured

City of San Diego, California, v. John Roe
(California Supreme Court)
Case No 03-1669 (2004)

INTRODUCTION

When John Roe, a San Diego police officer, decided he needed some additional income, he decided to go into the video production and distribution business in a not so conventional way. He made a video of himself stripping off his police uniform and masturbating. He then sold this video on eBay. In addition, he also sold custom videos, men's underwear, and police equipment, including official uniforms of the San Diego Police Department, via the site. His user profile on eBay also identified him as someone employed in the field of law enforcement.

When Roe's supervisor discovered his activities, an investigation was convened by the San Diego Police Department's (SDPD's) internal affairs division. In response to a request by an undercover officer, Roe produced a custom video which showed him issuing a traffic citation but revoking it after undoing his uniform and masturbating. When confronted with this evidence, Roe admitted to selling the videos and other police equipment.

The investigation report revealed that Roe had violated certain SDPD policies, including conduct becoming of an officer. He was ordered to "cease displaying, manufacturing, distributing, or selling any sexually explicit content or engaging in similar behaviors, via the Internet, U.S. mail, commercial vendors or distributors, or any other medium available to the public." Roe removed some of these items but continued to retain his eBay profile, which described the first two videos he produced along with their pricing as well as the prices for other custom videos.

Upon discovering that Roe had failed to follow its orders, the SDPD cited Roe for the added violation of disobedience of lawful orders and terminated him.

Roe then challenged his termination before the district court, arguing that his termination from employment was in violation of his First Amendment right to free speech. The district court sided with the City, holding that Roe had failed to demonstrate how the selling of police uniforms and sexually explicit videos for profit related to a matter of "public concern" requiring First Amendment protection. Roe, however, appealed this decision successfully at the court of appeals which held that his conduct did fall within the scope of citizen commentary on matters of public concern. In its decision, the court found that as Roe's expression was not an internal workplace grievance and occurred while he was off-duty and away from his workplace, it was unrelated to his employment, and the city's decision to terminate his services was in violation of his First Amendment right to free speech.

The city appealed this decision before the state Supreme Court.

WHAT THE COURT HELD

The California Supreme Court held in favor of the city of San Diego, reversing the court of appeals' findings. In coming to its decision, the court first deliberated on the issue of "under what circumstances can an employee's termination contravene his rights under the First Amendment," wherein it stated the following:

"There is no difficulty in concluding that Roe's expression does not qualify as a matter of public concern under any view of the public concern test. Roe's activities did nothing to inform the public about any aspect of the SDPD's functioning or operation. His expression was widely broadcast, linked to his official status as a police worker, and designed to exploit his employer's image. The speech in question was detrimental to the mission and functions of the employer. There is no basis for finding that it was of concern to the community as the court's cases have understood

that term in the context of restrictions by government entities on the speech of their employees."

HOW YOU CAN BENEFIT FROM THIS CASE

KNOW WHAT THE "PICKERING BALANCE" TEST REQUIRES

The Pickering Balance refers to the test emanating from the court decision in *Pickering v. Board of Education of Township High School District.* The test essentially seeks to balance the right of employers to impose certain restraints on the speech of their employees because of the employers' organizational interests, with the right of employees to speak on matters of public concern. In doing so, the first stage of the test that must be satisfied (under the Pickering Balance) is whether the speech involved a matter of public concern. Upon satisfying the test that it is a matter of public concern, the second stage of the test lies is determining which deserves greater protection, i.e., the employer's business interests (in seeking to restrain its employee's speech) or the public's right to know.

In Roe's case, he could not get past the first stage of this test, as he wasn't able to demonstrate how his speech or expression was a matter of public concern deserving First Amendment protection.

CASE 17

If your employer has multiple locations across the country, you need to know which state to sue under.

Case Featured

Hertz Corporation v. Friend et al.
(California Supreme Court)
Case No 08-1107 (2010)

INTRODUCTION

Many employers in the United States today have business locations in more than one state. Given this fact, what happens where you want to sue your employer for a state wage-and-hour-law-related violation? Where do you go? Do you sue the company in the state you work in, or do you sue it in the state where its corporate headquarters is located? Or do you sue it in the state where the majority of its business activities are conducted? This question has mystified and stymied the American judicial process for years and was finally decided via this landmark decision involving Hertz, the multinational car rental company.

In this featured case, Melinda Friend and John Nhieu, two Californian citizens, sued Hertz for wage and hour law violations in the California state court. In suing Hertz, they also requested relief on behalf of a potential class of California citizens that allegedly suffered similar harm by Hertz. Hertz, in response, filed a notice seeking to remove the case from state to federal court on the grounds that while Friend and Nhieu were from California, Hertz's principal place of business is New Jersey.

The district court, however, found that Hertz was a corporate citizen of California. In its decision, the district court found that the test for determining an employer's *"principal place of business"* is to first determine the employer's business activity state by state, and if the amount of activity is significantly larger in one particular state, then that state represents the company's *"principal place of business."*

As California accounted for almost one fifth of Hertz's revenue and workforce, the court found that it had jurisdiction over this case.

When the state court of appeals affirmed the district court's decision, Hertz launched its appeal before the state Supreme Court.

WHAT THE COURT HELD

The Supreme Court for the State of California found in favor of Hertz, ruling that the correct test to determine the site of a corporation's principal place of business is to use the *"nerve center"* test, which refers to identifying where the location of the corporation's main center of control, command, and coordination is. It accordingly quoted the following in stating its decision that Hertz's principal place of business was New Jersey:

"We conclude that 'principal place of business' is best read as referring to the place where the corporation's officers direct, control, and coordinate the corporation's activities. It is the place that the Court of Appeals have called the corporation's 'nerve-center.' And in practice it should normally be the place where the corporation maintains its headquarters – provided that the headquarters is the actual center of direction, control and coordination, and not simply an office where the corporation holds its board meetings (for example, attended by directors and officers who have traveled there for the occasion)."

The court also quoted the following important observation in relation to why it favored the "nerve center" approach over the "significant business activities" approach earlier advocated by the district court and court of appeals:

"A corporation's 'nerve center,' usually its main headquarters, is a single place. The public often (though not always) considers it the corporation's main place of business. And it is a place within a state. By contrast, the application of a more general business activities test has led some courts, as in the present case, to look, not at a particular place within a state, but incorrectly at the state itself, measuring the total amount of business activities

that the corporation conducts there and determining whether they are 'significantly larger' than in the next ranking state.

This approach invites greater litigation and can lead to strange results, as the Ninth Circuit has since recognized. Namely, if a 'corporation may be deemed to be a citizen of California on the basis of activities that roughly reflect California's largest population...nearly every national retailer—no matter how far flung its operations—will be deemed a citizen of California for diversity purposes."

HOW YOU CAN BENEFIT FROM THIS CASE

CLARITY ON HOW TO IDENTIFY AN EMPLOYER'S PRINCIPAL PLACE OF BUSINESS

This court decision has hopefully now put an end to the unfortunate gamesmanship sometimes displayed by larger organizations in frustrating employee suits. The "nerve center" approach is the test adopted in determining an employer's principal place of business.

HOW TO DETERMINE WHICH IS YOUR EMPLOYER'S NERVE CENTER

Simple. Think of your employer's nerve center as its base of "overall direction, control, and coordination." Another way is to ask this straightforward question:

"Where is my organization's base of command?"

CASE 18

Your local union has a right to collect "service fees" from you despite your not being a member.

Case Featured

Locke et al. v. Karass, State Controller, et al.
(The United States Supreme Court)
Case No 07-610 (2009)

INTRODUCTION

After the state of Maine designated the Maine State Employees Association (the local union) as the exclusive bargaining agent for certain executive branch employees, a collective bargaining agreement was signed between the state and the local union which required non-union members to pay a "service fee." This service fee was established by deducting, on a prorated basis, nonchargeable union activities such as political, public relations, or lobbying activities from the ordinary union dues paid by members. It also included a charge for affiliation fees paid by the local union to its national union, the Service Employees International Union—fees which were in turn used to help the national union pay its litigation expenses.

The nonunion members were upset at having to pay these service fees, in particular the affiliation fees to pay for litigation costs incurred by the national union. Their main ground for contention was that they, as nonmembers, shouldn't be made to bear part of these litigation costs since they brought no direct benefit to the local union.

When both the district court and court of appeals held in favor of the state union, the nonunion members challenged this decision at the state Supreme Court.

WHAT THE COURT HELD

The Supreme Court affirmed the court of appeals decision, finding that the state union had a right to charge nonunionized employees for national litigation expenses. In basing its decision on this issue, the court stated the following:

"We can find no sound basis for holding that national social activities, national convention activities, and activities involved in producing the non-political portions of national union publications are chargeable but national litigation expenses are not. Of course, a local non-member presumably has the right to attend, and consequently can benefit from, national social and convention activities; and a local non-member can read, and benefit from, a national publication. But so can a local non-member benefit from national litigation aimed at helping other units if the national or other units will similarly contribute to the cost of litigation on the local union's behalf should the need arise."

HOW YOU CAN BENEFIT FROM THE CASE

KNOW THE "LEHNER STANDARD" ON WHAT YOUR UNION CAN AND CANNOT CHARGE YOU FOR IF YOU'RE A NONUNION MEMBER

The "Lehner standard" says that in evaluating a local union's right to charge a nonmember for its national union's litigation fees, it must be able to demonstrate that the charges are for:

1) the *direct* costs of negotiating and administering a collective bargaining contract; or
2) services that may ultimately benefit the local union by virtue of their membership in the national union.

If you're able to demonstrate that either of these two requirements is not met, you could challenge these charges. Bear in mind, though, that the courts are inclined to take a liberal approach in giving unions latitude to pursue actions or causes they feel are in the best interest of their members.

CASE 19

"Noncompete" agreements must be specific, reasonable, and fair to the employee.

Case Featured

Speciality Rental Tools & Supply, LP v. William P. Shoemaker, Senior (U.S. Court of Appeals for the Fifth Circuit) Case No 08-60061 (2009)

INTRODUCTION

When Speciality Rental Tools & Supply purchased Shoemaker's firm, Southeastern Rentals, it entered into an agreement with Shoemaker to hire him under a five-year employment contract. As part of the deal, Shoemaker also signed an agreement not to compete, valid for two years from the date he entered into the purchase agreement.

When his employment contract expired five years later, STS sent Shoemaker a letter informing him that they would not be renewing the employment relationship. Shoemaker left and then went to work for a direct competitor of STS, leading STS to file a lawsuit restraining Shoemaker from competing against it. When the district court found in Shoemaker's favor, STS appealed before the present court of appeals.

WHAT THE COURTS HELD

The United States Court of Appeals found in favor of Shoemaker. In finding for Shoemaker in his case against STS, the court stated that restraint-of-trade clauses are generally not looked upon favorably by the law unless they are *reasonable* and *specific* in terms of what they prohibit. In finding that Shoemaker's restraint-of-trade terms were neither specific nor reasonable, the court stated the following:

"In more narrowly framing its task, the district court quoted the Mississippi Supreme Court's pronouncement that 'restrictive

covenants are in restraint of trade and individual freedom and are not favorites of the law.' It emphasized that the enforceability of such agreements is largely predicated upon the reasonableness and specificity of its terms."

The court also addressed the issue of whether Shoemaker's agreement not to compete was valid for two years or for the five years of his employment contract where it found that the restraint of trade clause was only valid for two years. It accordingly stated:

"As STS lost its entitlement to enforce the non-competition agreement's covenant when it expired on March 1, 2004, with Shoemaker still employed there, STS was left with the Purchase Agreement's covenant 'not to compete' as its only potential enforcement mechanism. But, after the March 1, 2004 anniversary of the signing of the Purchase Agreement, its covenant could be enforced only if a termination of Shoemaker's employment with STS occurred during the years of its five-year term. And, as this condition precedent occurred, the Purchase Agreement's covenant against competition expired, simultaneously with the expiration of the Employment Agreement, on March 1, 2007."

HOW YOU CAN BENEFIT FROM THIS CASE

AGREEMENTS NOT TO COMPETE ARE ENFORCEABLE PROVIDED THEY ARE SPECIFIC AND REASONABLE

The good news for employees is that your employer can't issue you a blanket noncompete agreement prohibiting you from using your gained experience, skills, and expertise for any future employment endeavors. An example of a blanket noncompete agreement is where a computer systems analyst is asked to sign an "agreement not to compete" stipulating that he or she cannot work within the information technology industry upon ceasing employment with your employer. Here, the courts are likely to disregard such noncompete agreements as unreasonable and too general, rendering them invalid.

However, if you are instrumental in the development process of a cutting-edge software technology with your former employer and had confidential insight into its process and proprietary systems design, an agreement not to compete could be held enforceable when you leave to take up a position with this former employer's direct competitor, *provided* your employer stipulates which companies you are prohibited from joining, the geographical area you are prohibited from competing in, and the time frame.

As a general rule, the courts are reluctant to enforce agreements not to compete as they conflict with a person's right to seek a livelihood. After all, shouldn't a person be allowed to benefit from the work experience he or she gained to better his or her career prospects? The courts will therefore strive to balance these two diverging interests, i.e., an employer's need for protection against an employee's right to seek a living.

CASE 20

Your pension fund can't vary your pension terms once you've retired.

Case Featured

Central Laborers' Pension Fund v. Heinz et al.
(The United States Supreme Court)
Case No 02-891 (2004)

CASE OVERVIEW

Heinz and a group of others who were retired participated in the Central Laborers' Pension Fund, a multiemployer pension fund. After accruing enough pension credits to qualify for early retirement, Heinz retired. When he retired, the pension plan had a clause on what constituted work that would disqualify him from enjoying his pension— called "disqualifying employment." This "disqualifying employment" included construction worker jobs but did not include "supervisory" roles—one of which Heinz later took up.

After his retirement, the plan expanded its criteria for disqualifying employment to include all jobs in construction, including supervisory positions. When Heinz refused to leave his supervisory position, the fund stopped his payment. Heinz then sued to recover these suspended benefits, claiming that the suspension violated the "anti-cutback" rule under the Employee Retirement Income Security Act (ERISA), which prohibits any pension plan amendment that would reduce a participant's accrued benefit.

The district court, however, found in favor of the Central Laborers' Pension Fund. Heinz appealed and the Seventh Circuit of the U.S. Court of Appeals reversed the district court's decision, leading to the fund appealing this decision before the Supreme Court.

WHAT THE COURT HELD

The United States Supreme Court found in favor of Heinz, ruling that ERISA prohibits a plan amendment that:

1.   expands the categories of "disqualifying employment" for postretirees; and
2.   triggers the suspension of payments to early retirement benefits already accrued.

In its decision in favor of Heinz, the court quoted the following:

"The anti-cutback provision is crucial to ERISA's central object of protecting employees' justified expectations of receiving the benefits that they have been promised. The provision prohibits plan amendments that have 'the effect of...eliminating or reducing an early retirement benefit.' The question here is whether the Plan's amendment had such an effect. Although the statutory text is not as helpful as it might be, it is clear as a matter of common sense that a benefit has suffered under the amendment. Heinz accrued benefits under a plan allowing him to supplement his retirement income, and he reasonably relied on that plan's terms in planning his retirement. The 1998 amendment undercut that reliance, paying benefits only if he accepted a substantial curtailment of his opportunity to do the work he knew. There is no way that, in any practical sense, this change in terms could not be viewed as shrinking the value of Heinz's pension rights and reducing his promised benefits."

HOW YOU CAN BENEFIT FROM THIS CASE

NEW CONDITIONS IMPOSED BY A PENSION PLAN CANNOT AFFECT ANY BENEFIT THAT YOU HAVE ALREADY EARNED OR ACCRUED

ERISA's objective is to protect employees' justified expectation that upon retirement, they will receive the benefits that have been promised to them. While your employer is not required by law to establish a pension plan, ERISA does mandate the terms an employer must fulfill once it decides to have a plan—including ensuring that it does not impose a new condition affecting any benefit you have already earned or accrued. A relevant quote by the court here on this matter is seen below:

> *"Nothing in ERISA requires employers to establish employee benefits plans. Nor does ERISA mandate what kind of benefits employers must provide if they choose to have such a plan. ERISA does, however, seek to ensure that employees will not be left empty-handed once employers have guaranteed them certain benefits... When Congress enacted ERISA, it wanted to make sure that if a worker has been promised a defined pension benefit upon retirement—and he has fulfilled whatever conditions are required to obtain the vested benefit—he actually receives it." (from* **Lockheed v. Speed,** *quoting* **Nachman Corp v. Pension Benefit Guarantee Corporation).***

CASE 21

Your employer may have created exceptions to its 'employment at will' policy.

Case Featured

Huey v. Honeywell, Inc.
(The United States Court of Appeals, Ninth Circuit)
Case No 94-15748 (1996)

INTRODUCTION

When Honeywell suspected one of its employees, John Huey, of abusing its flextime policy, it commenced investigations that included conducting surveillance of his home and obtaining personal information about his wife and family. Neither Huey nor his supervisor was ever questioned. Two months later, Huey was summarily terminated by Honeywell using the "employment at will" policy contained in its employee manual stating:

"Employment at Honeywell, Inc. is voluntarily entered into and employees are free to resign at anytime. Similarly, Honeywell may terminate the employment relationship where it believes it is in the company's best interests. The policy statements contained in this manual do not intend to negate this principle."

However, this policy was not communicated to Huey by his supervisor. This led to Huey suing for unfair termination. The district court, however, held that Honeywell had a right to terminate him using its "employment at will" policy, leading to Huey's present appeal before the federal court of appeals.

WHAT THE COURT HELD

The U.S. Court of Appeals for the Ninth Circuit reversed the district court's decision, ruling that Honeywell was wrong to apply its "employment at will" principle in terminating Huey. In its decision, the court found that Honeywell had, via certain actions and policies, contradicted its right to treat Huey as an "at-will" employee. It accordingly quoted the following:

> *"The following actions by Honeywell created a material question of fact as to Huey's employment status as an 'at will' employee: (1) Honeywell developed written policies and a personnel manual adopting a progressive disciplinary program; (2) Honeywell relies on its supervisors to orally explain its personnel policies to other employees; (3) Honeywell's written policies and personnel manual were not distributed to its employees; (4) Although the personnel manual contained a disclaimer which stated that no portion of the manual was to be interpreted as altering Honeywell's at will employment contracts, this waiver was not orally relayed to Huey and he was not given a copy of the manual; and (5) Huey was aware of other employees at Honeywell who were progressively disciplined, rather than terminated, for violating company policies.*

> *"If an employer does not choose to issue a policy statement, in a manual or otherwise, and by its language or by the employer's actions, encourages reliance thereon, the employer cannot be free to only selectively abide by it. Having announced a policy, the employer may not treat it as illusory. Honeywell clearly chose to issue a policy statement and it would practice progressive discipline by setting forth such a policy in its manual and relying upon its supervisors to relay its policy to other employees. Therefore, Honeywell may not treat this policy as illusory."*

HOW YOU CAN BENEFIT FROM THIS CASE

I. THE THREE EMPLOYMENT-AT-WILL EXCEPTIONS

While your employer is generally free to decide if it wants to structure the employment relationship on an at-will basis, there are three exceptions to this principle:

a) It cannot be in conflict with any public policy, be it a city ordinance or state or federal law. For instance, your employer cannot dismiss you for reporting shareholder fraud under Sarbanes-Oxley—this is a federal law, henceforth a matter of public policy.

b)   If your employer has created an "implied promise" of permanent or long-term employment, you could claim that, by implication, you cannot be terminated on an at-will basis—for instance, if your superior informs you in writing, "You've got a job here as long as you want it."

c)   If your employer has created an implied promise to treat you "in good faith and fairly"—for instance, if your company's disciplinary process provides that prior to termination, you will be accorded with due process via a series of verbal and written warnings

In Honeywell's case, the court found that the fact that it had established progressive discipline procedures which it had used to counsel other employees created an "implied promise" that Huey, too, could not simply be terminated without first going through the company's disciplinary process.

2. NEGOTIATE TERMS BEFORE YOU JOIN YOUR EMPLOYER

Employers, too, want to attract the right caliber employees, and, in doing so, need to make the job attractive to prospective applicants. The best time to negotiate the terms of your contract is during the prehiring stage, when the employer would be more amenable to your terms. Use this opportunity to negotiate for your right to be terminated only for justifiable reasons (just cause) and after you have been accorded the right to be heard (due process).

When negotiating for this right, you could point to the reality that all you're asking is to be treated fairly!

CASE 22

Same sex harassment is still protected under Title VII coverage.

Case Featured

Oncale v. Sundowner Offshore Services, Inc.
(The Supreme Court of the United States)
Case No 95-568 (1998)

INTRODUCTION

Oncale, a married man with kids, worked for Sundowner Offshore Services on its oil platform in the Gulf of Mexico. He worked with an eight-men crew which included John Lyons, Danny Pippen, and Brandon Johnson, with Lyons and Pippen having supervisory authority over him.

Oncale brought forth an allegation that on several occasions, Lyons, Pippen, and Johnson subjected him to sex-related, humiliating actions in the presence of other crew members—including threatening him with rape. When no action was taken by his superiors despite him raising the issue, Oncale resigned and requested that his pink slip state he "voluntarily left due to sexual harassment and verbal abuse." He then sued Sundowner and the others, alleging sex discrimination.

Both the district court and court of appeals, however, held that Oncale's complaint had no Title VII (of the Civil Rights Act) applicability, as he was alleging sexual harassment by co-workers who were of the same gender or sex. Oncale challenged this decision before the Supreme Court.

WHAT THE COURT HELD

The Supreme Court of the United States held in favor of Oncale, finding that same-sex harassment claims are covered by Title VII. In its decision on this issue, the court stated the following:

> *"We see no justification in the statutory language or our precedents for a categorical rule excluding same-sex harassment claims from the coverage of Title VII. As some courts have observed, male on male sexual harassment in the workplace was assuredly not the principal evil Congress was concerned with when it enacted Title VII. But statutory prohibitions often go beyond the principal evil to cover reasonably comparable evils, and it is ultimately the provisions of our laws rather than the principal concerns of our legislators by which we are governed. Title VII prohibits discrimination because of sex in the terms and conditions of employment. Our holding that this includes sexual harassment must extend to sexual harassment of any kind that meets the statutory requirement."*

HOW YOU CAN BENEFIT FROM THIS CASE

TITLE VII COVERS ALL FORMS OF SEXUAL HARASSMENT

Sexual harassment needn't originate from members of the opposite sex to attract Title VII protection. Male on male, female on female, and even transgender-related discrimination are forms of sexual harassment that are actionable under Title VII. While some may argue that this decision transforms Title VII into a "general civility code" for the American workplace, the fact that it has now been decided upon by the courts demonstrates that your employer cannot dismiss the reality that same-sex discrimination does happen and needs to be addressed.

The Author

Shawn Sher is the president and CEO of Lyons Shers Incorporated, an international industrial relations specialist advising multinational corporations and individuals on their rights, responsibilities, and obligations with people and work. Lyons Shers's chief mission is the promotion of equity or fairness at the workplace.